WISE WORDS FROM LEFT-HANDERS

A COLORING BOOK FOR ADULTS

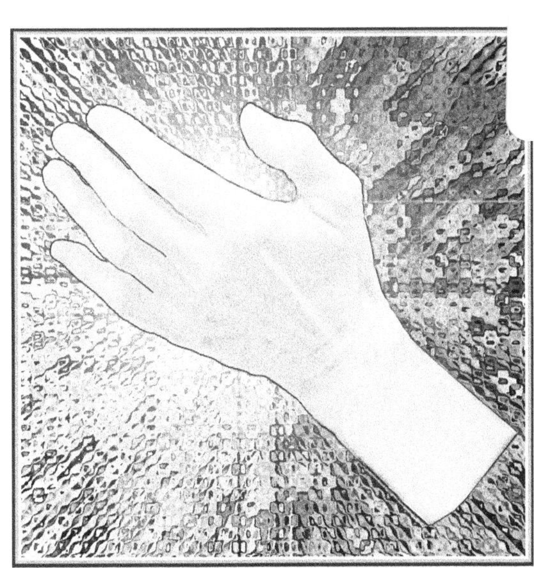

K. SHERRERD LOWRY

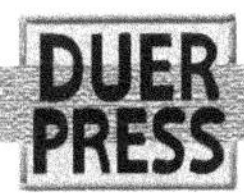

ISBN-10: 1-945939-00-1

ISBN-13: 978-1-945939-00-6

Published by Duer Press

www.duerpress.com

Printed in the United States of America

A Few Words of Introduction

The phenomenon of coloring as a pursuit for adults continues to grow. The reason: the benefits become apparent almost immediately. Coloring affects the brain as other mindfulness exercises do; there is a calm that accompanies the simple act of busying the hands while disengaging the mind from troubles and worries.

The first book in this series, *Wise Words from Shakespeare: A Coloring Book for Adults*, was inspired by my own wish for choices in coloring material beyond the usual abstract-graphic collections. Coloring an abstract figure or drawing is gratifying and effective in focusing the mind on the present moment—but so, too, is coloring a picture that represents an interesting person, place, or thing. A love of Shakespeare's language guided the selection of topic for that first book. To illustrate those wise words, I found myself wanting to incorporate period sources—oil paintings, woodcuts, etchings—into my pictures.

This new book follows the same plan. The pictures depart from the standard black-lines-around-white-spaces found in standard children's coloring books, by reflecting the modeling and dimensionality found in the original sources.

This book arose from two sources: feedback from people who had enjoyed the first book, and the fact that I grew up as the child of a left-handed parent. All such children soon realize that the world is, largely, arranged for the convenience of the right-handed. Coloring books for adults increasingly are made with blank pages on the reverse of each graphic page, to prevent bleed-through of colors—but of course those graphics appear on *right*-hand pages. Equal time for the convenience of the left-handed seems only fair! (Given the demands of publishing, the covers and front and back matter for this volume are in the conventional format—but the quotations and pictures do appear on the left.) It's my hope that both left-handed and right-handed people will enjoy using this book.

History is filled with notable left-handed people. I have gone back only as far as 1706 (the birth of Benjamin Franklin) because for those famous people of antiquity who we believe to have been left-handed, the question of handedness is sometimes only an unconfirmed guess. For people alive in the last three centuries, we can be more certain. And there are so many accomplished, brilliant, and significant left-handers from which to choose! Their advice is timeless.

Timeless advice is always of interest, and making art using famous quotations is a popular pastime. But the sad fact is that a large proportion of the quotes found on Internet sites were never said or written by the person to whom they're attributed. Sometimes the misattributions are rather comical, as when Shakespeare is credited with a remark about using an umbrella. (Umbrellas did not appear in England until more than a century after the Bard's death.) To avoid such incongruity, I relied heavily on sources dedicated to getting sourcing right, such as Wikiquote.org and quoteinvestigator.com. The quotations chosen for this book are all well-sourced.

In using any coloring book, it is advisable to place a plain piece of paper (or two) under the page being colored. The inks used for the book itself can vary in the printing process, and the coloring instruments used can bleed through. A shield-paper will prevent any ink being transferred to the next picture in the book. (Many felt-tip markers are particularly likely to show through to the next page.)

As I said in the Shakespeare book: the most important thing to remember is that *you can't get this wrong*. What you create is yours—as is the satisfaction to be found in becoming immersed in the delights of coloring. Enjoy!

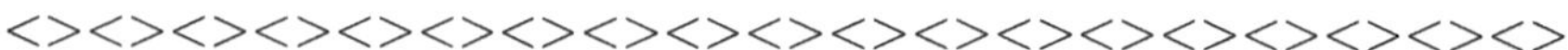

STUDY AND IN GENERAL THE PURSUIT OF TRUTH AND BEAUTY IS A SPHERE OF ACTIVITY IN WHICH WE ARE PERMITTED TO REMAIN CHILDREN ALL OUR LIVES.

--- ALBERT EINSTEIN: Letter to Adrianna Enriques (October 1921), p. 83

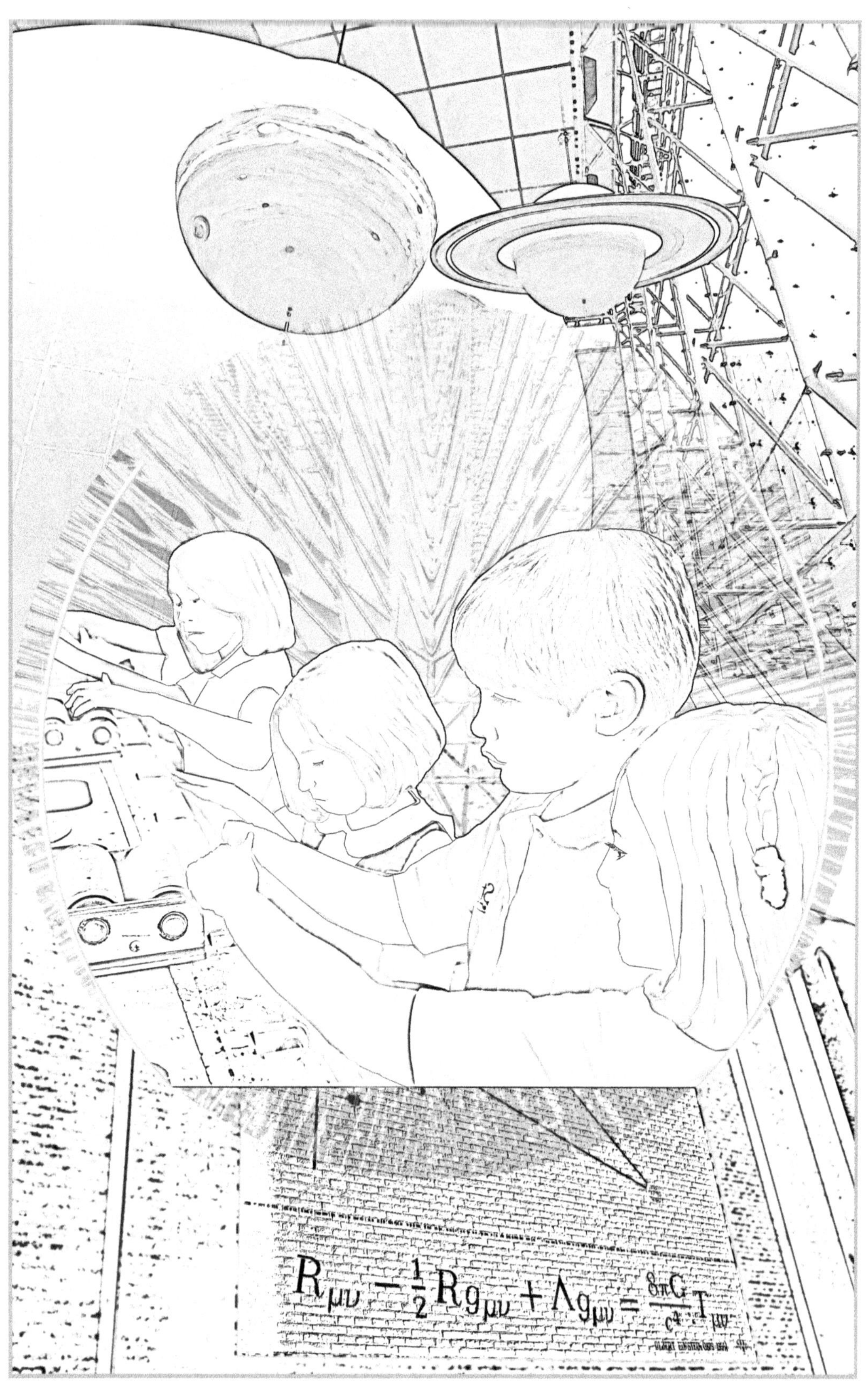
$R_{\mu\nu} - \frac{1}{2}Rg_{\mu\nu} + \Lambda g_{\mu\nu} = \frac{8\pi G}{c^4}T_{\mu\nu}$

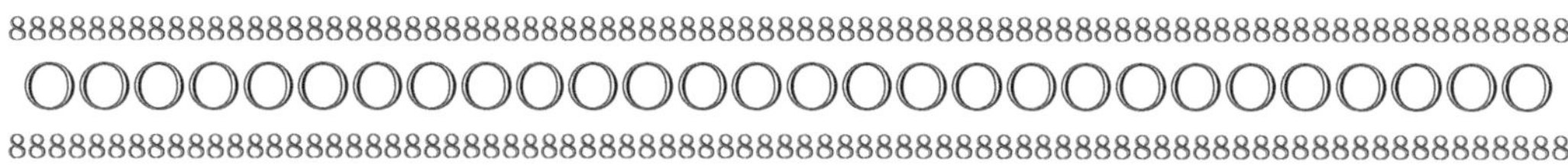

ALWAYS BE A FIRST-RATE VERSION OF YOURSELF, INSTEAD OF A SECOND-RATE VERSION OF SOMEBODY ELSE.

– JUDY GARLAND: As quoted in *Business Etiquette for the Nineties : Your Ticket to Career Success* (1992) by Lou Kennedy, p. 8

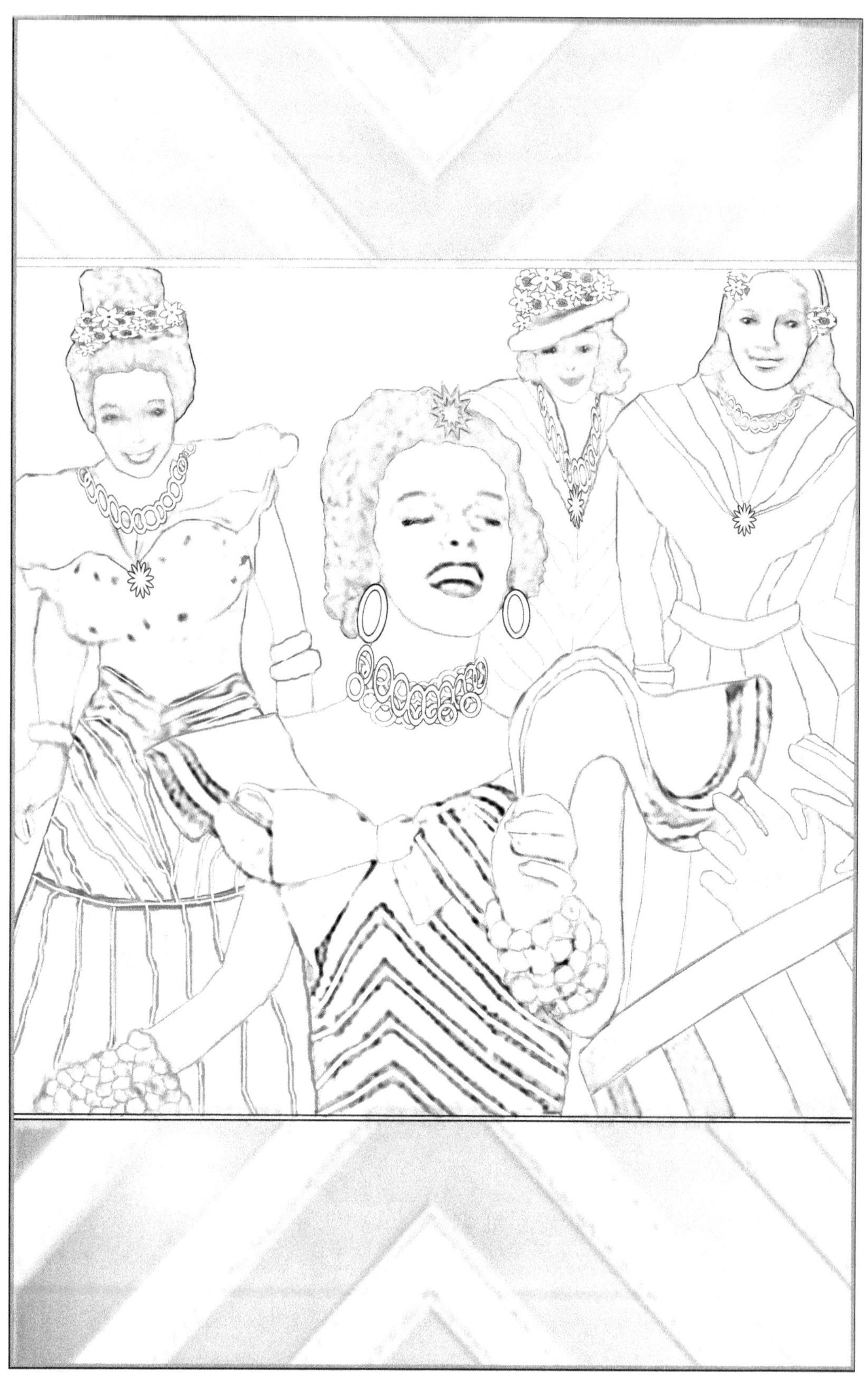

ALL I INSIST ON, AND NOTHING ELSE, IS THAT YOU SHOULD SHOW THE WHOLE WORLD THAT YOU ARE NOT AFRAID. BE SILENT, IF YOU CHOOSE; BUT WHEN IT IS NECESSARY, SPEAK—AND SPEAK IN SUCH A WAY THAT PEOPLE WILL REMEMBER IT.

– WOLFGANG AMADEUS MOZART: Letter as published in The Letters of Mozart & His Family (1938) translated and edited by Emily Anderson, p. 1114.

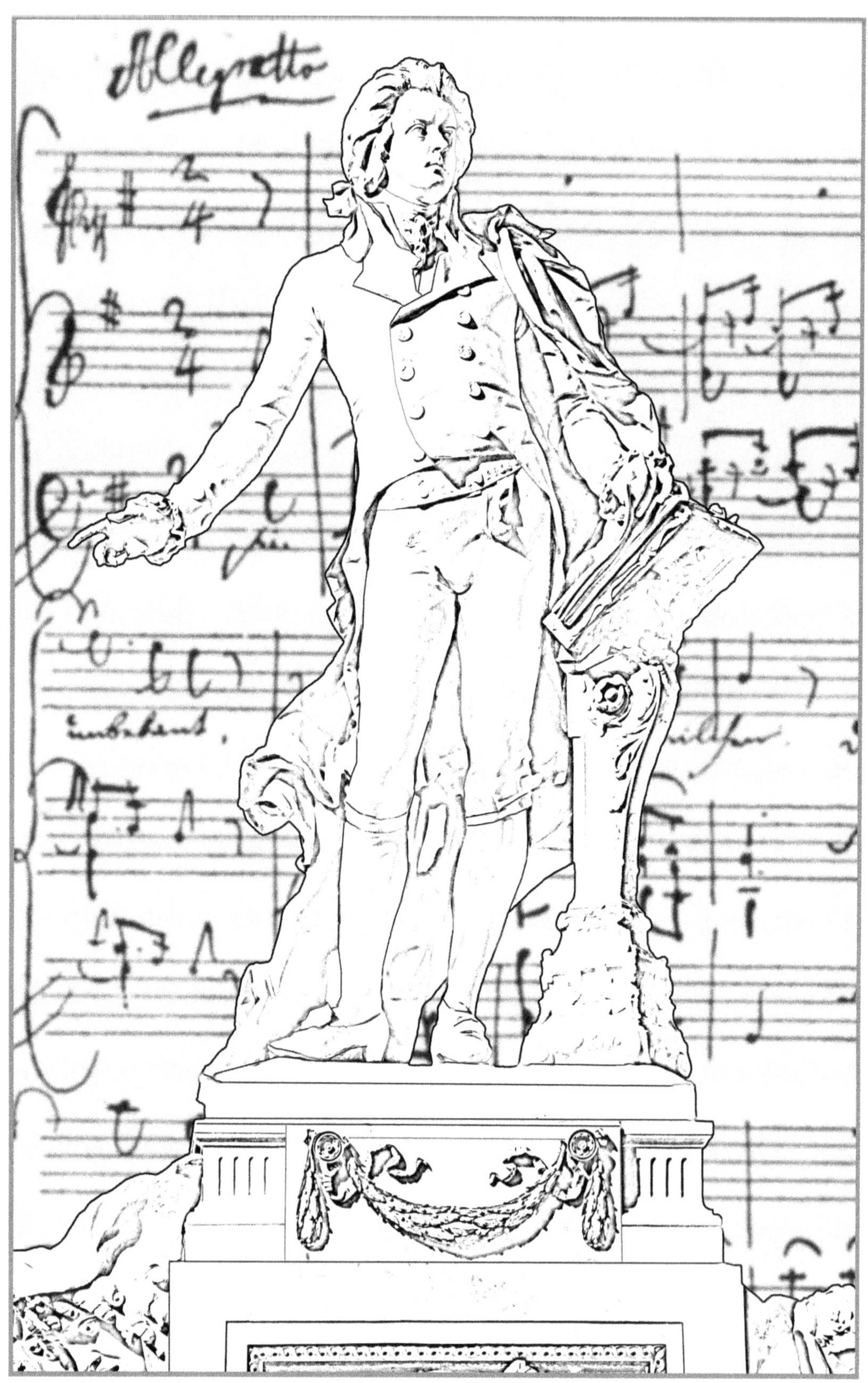
Allegretto

WE ARE NOT INTERESTED IN THE POSSIBILITIES OF DEFEAT; THEY DO NOT EXIST.

– QUEEN VICTORIA: December 1899 letter to Arthur Balfour during the "Black Week" of the Boer War, as quoted in The Columbia Dictionary of Quotations (1993), p. 539

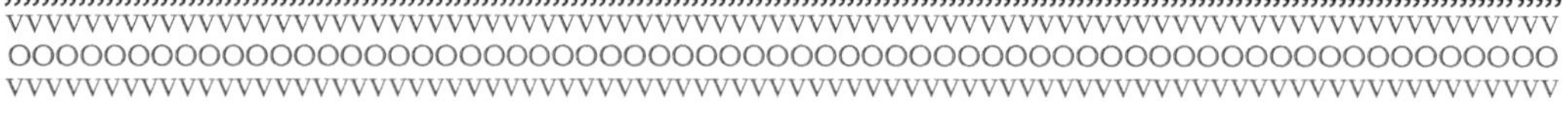

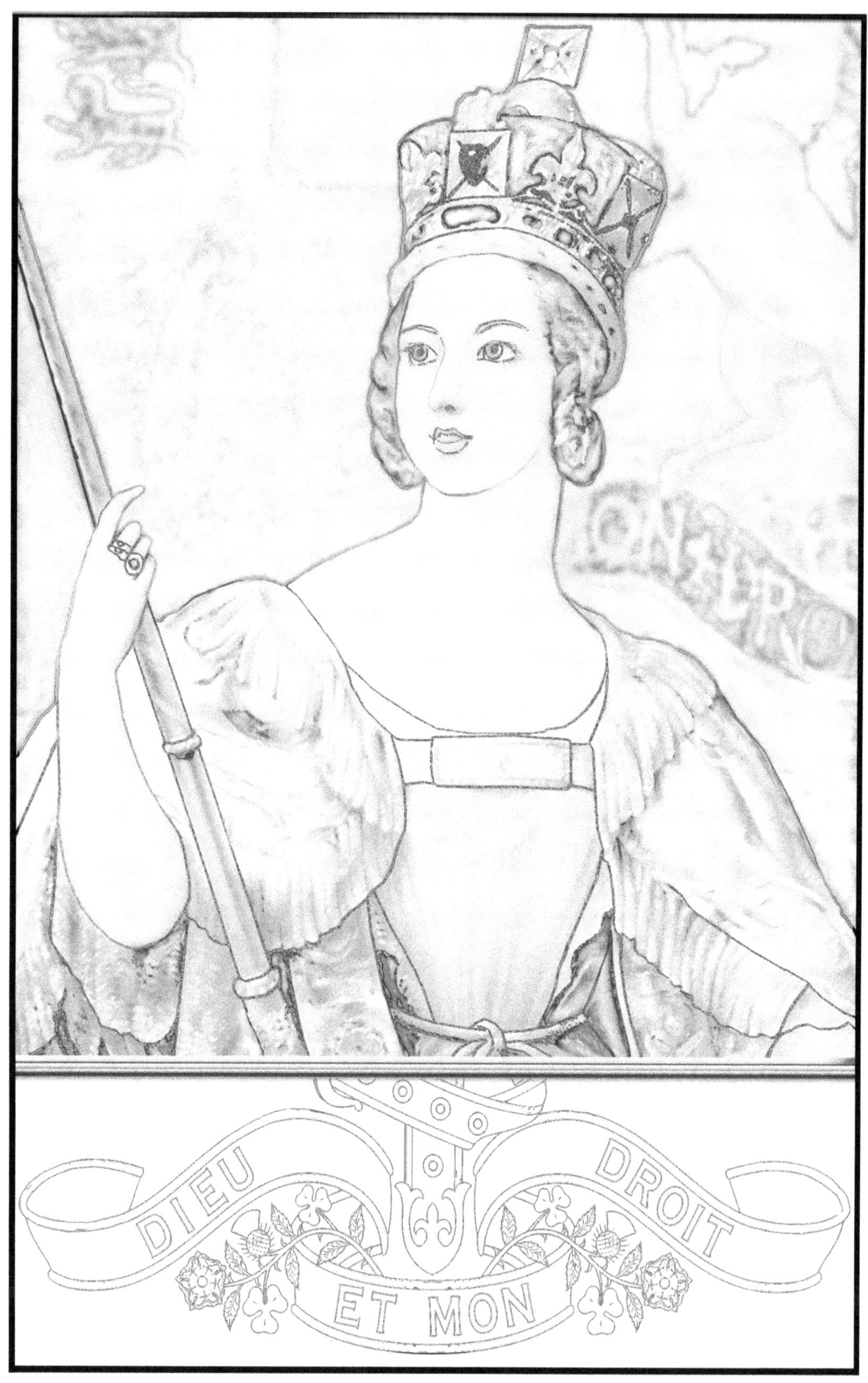
DIEU
DROIT
ET MON

I DON'T BELIEVE IN ANTI-ANYTHING. A MAN HAS TO HAVE A PROGRAM; YOU HAVE TO BE FOR SOMETHING, OTHERWISE YOU WILL NEVER GET ANYWHERE.

--- HARRY S. TRUMAN: Lecture at Columbia University (28 April 1959)

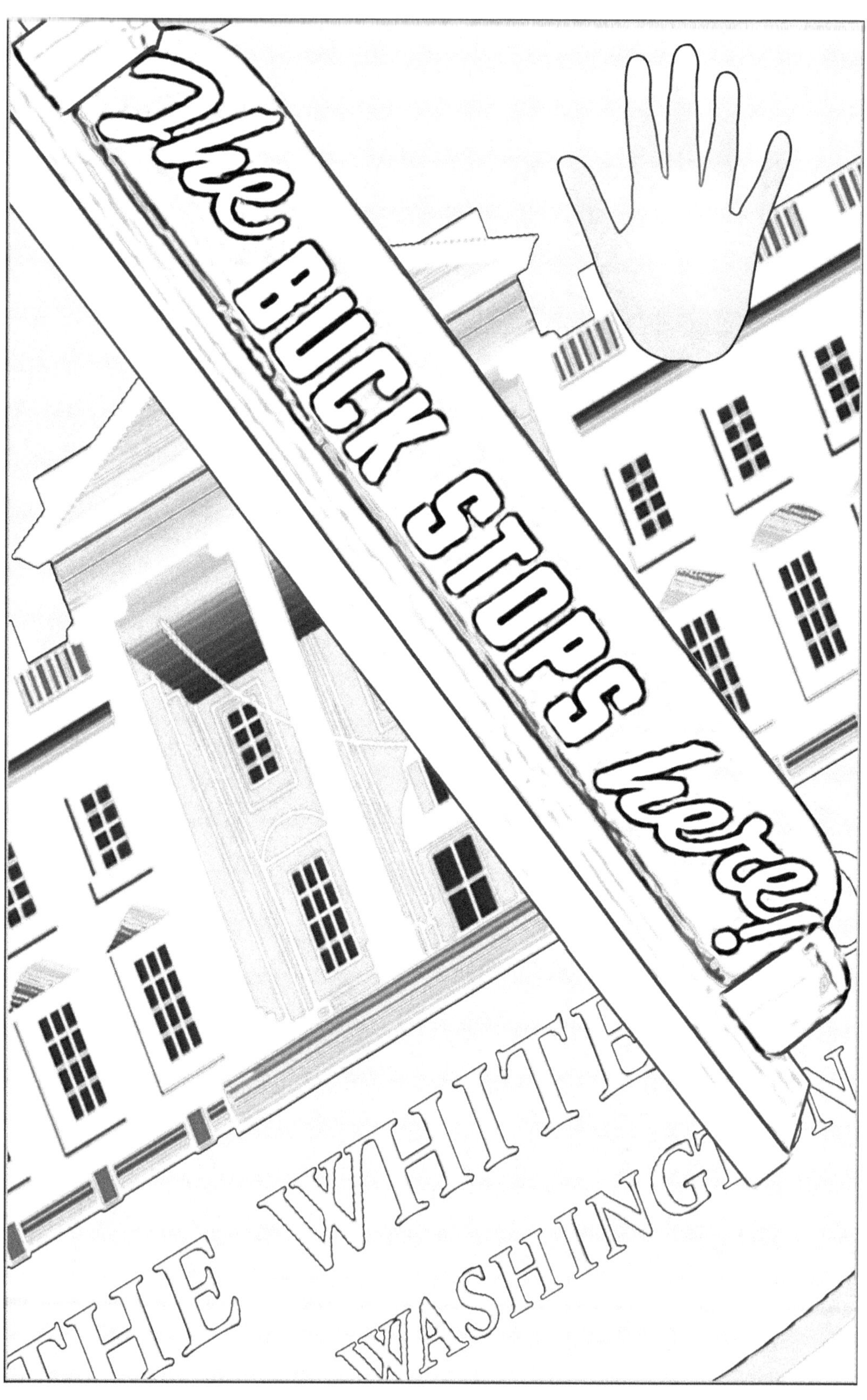
The BUCK STOPS here!
THE WHITE

"TO ME, ONE OF THE MOST BEAUTIFUL THINGS TO SEE IS A GROUP OF MEN COORDINATING THEIR EFFORTS TOWARD A COMMON GOAL, ALTERNATELY SUBORDINATING AND ASSERTING THEMSELVES TO ACHIEVE REAL TEAMWORK IN ACTION."

--- BILL RUSSELL: quoted in article at http://www.nba.com/history/players/russell_bio.html

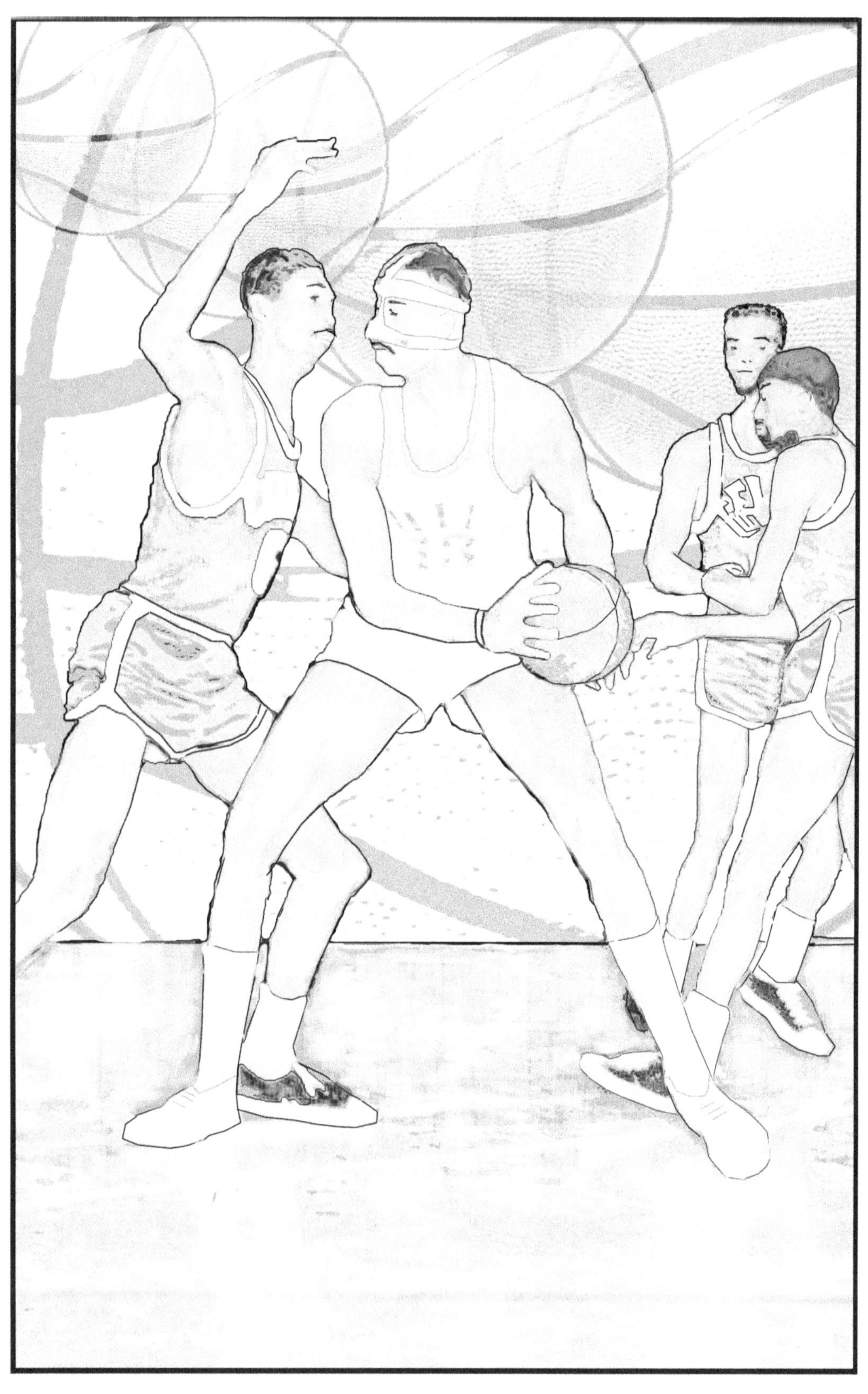

IF YOU WANT TO INSPIRE CONFIDENCE, GIVE PLENTY OF STATISTICS – IT DOES NOT MATTER THAT THEY SHOULD BE ACCURATE, OR EVEN INTELLIGIBLE, SO LONG AS THERE IS ENOUGH OF THEM.

--- LEWIS CARROLL (Charles L. Dodgson): Three Years in a Curatorship, By One Whom It Has Tried, 1886.

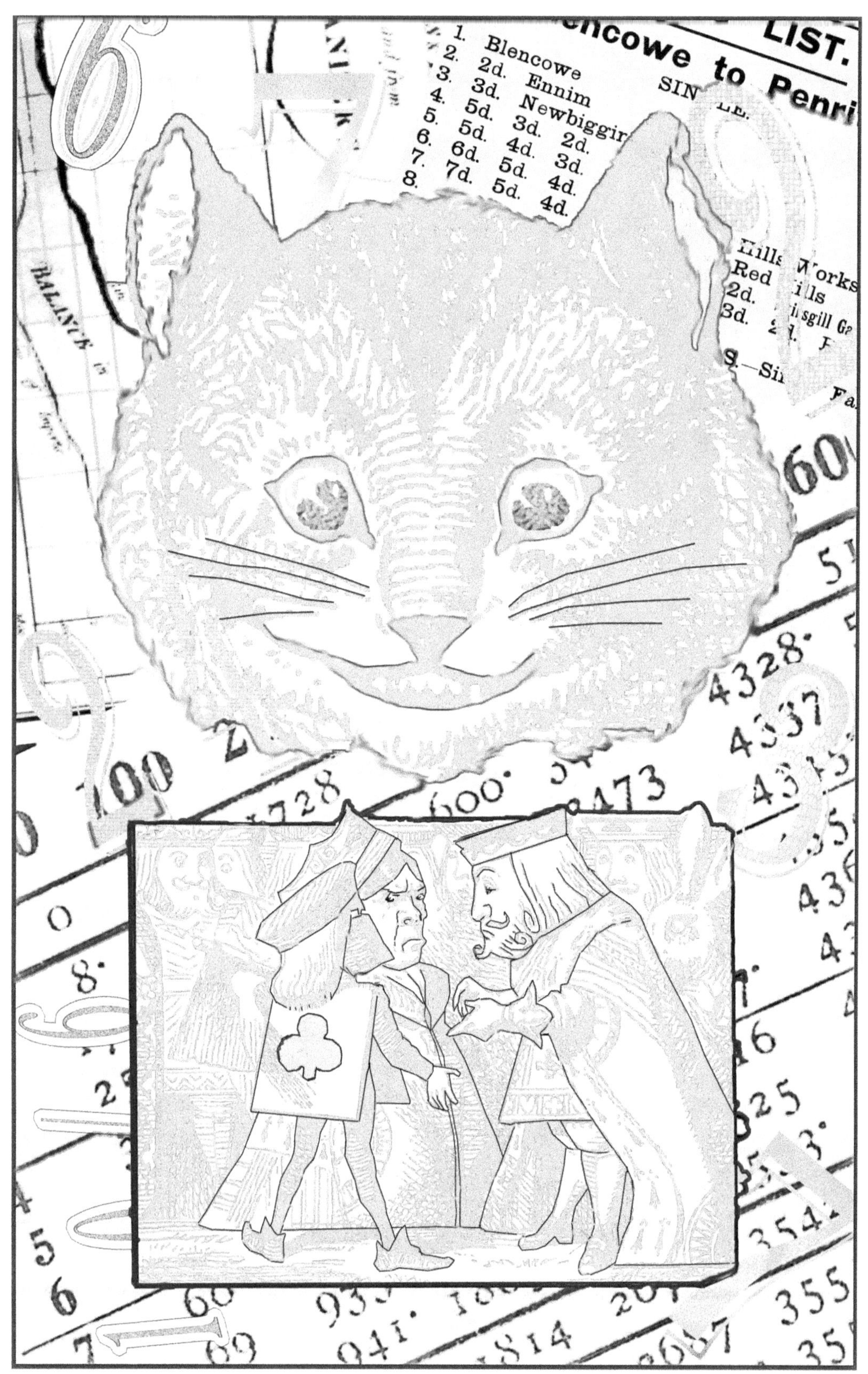

LIST.
1. Blencowe
2. 2d. Ennim
5. 5d. 3d. 2d.
6. 5d. 4d. 3d.
7. 6d. 5d. 4d.
8. 7d. 5d. 4d. 4d.
Red
4328
600
473

NOTHING IN LIFE IS TO BE FEARED, IT IS ONLY TO BE UNDERSTOOD. NOW IS THE TIME TO UNDERSTAND MORE, SO THAT WE MAY FEAR LESS.

– MARIE CURIE: As quoted in Our Precarious Habitat (1973) by Melvin A. Benarde, p. v

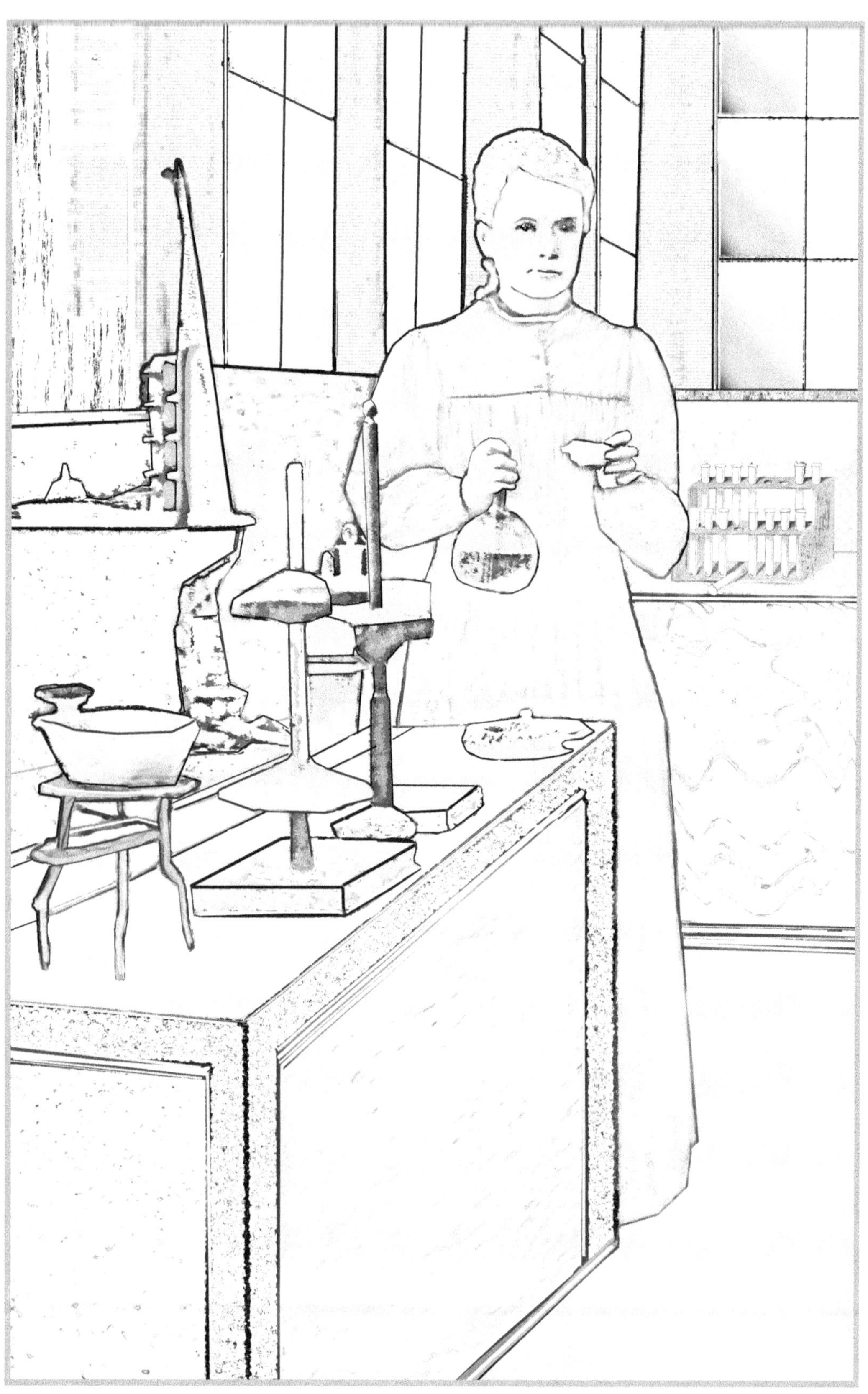

THINKING IS THE HARDEST WORK THERE IS, WHICH IS PROBABLY THE REASON WHY SO FEW ENGAGE IN IT.

--- HENRY FORD: As quoted in The High School Teacher, Vol. XI (1935), p. 60

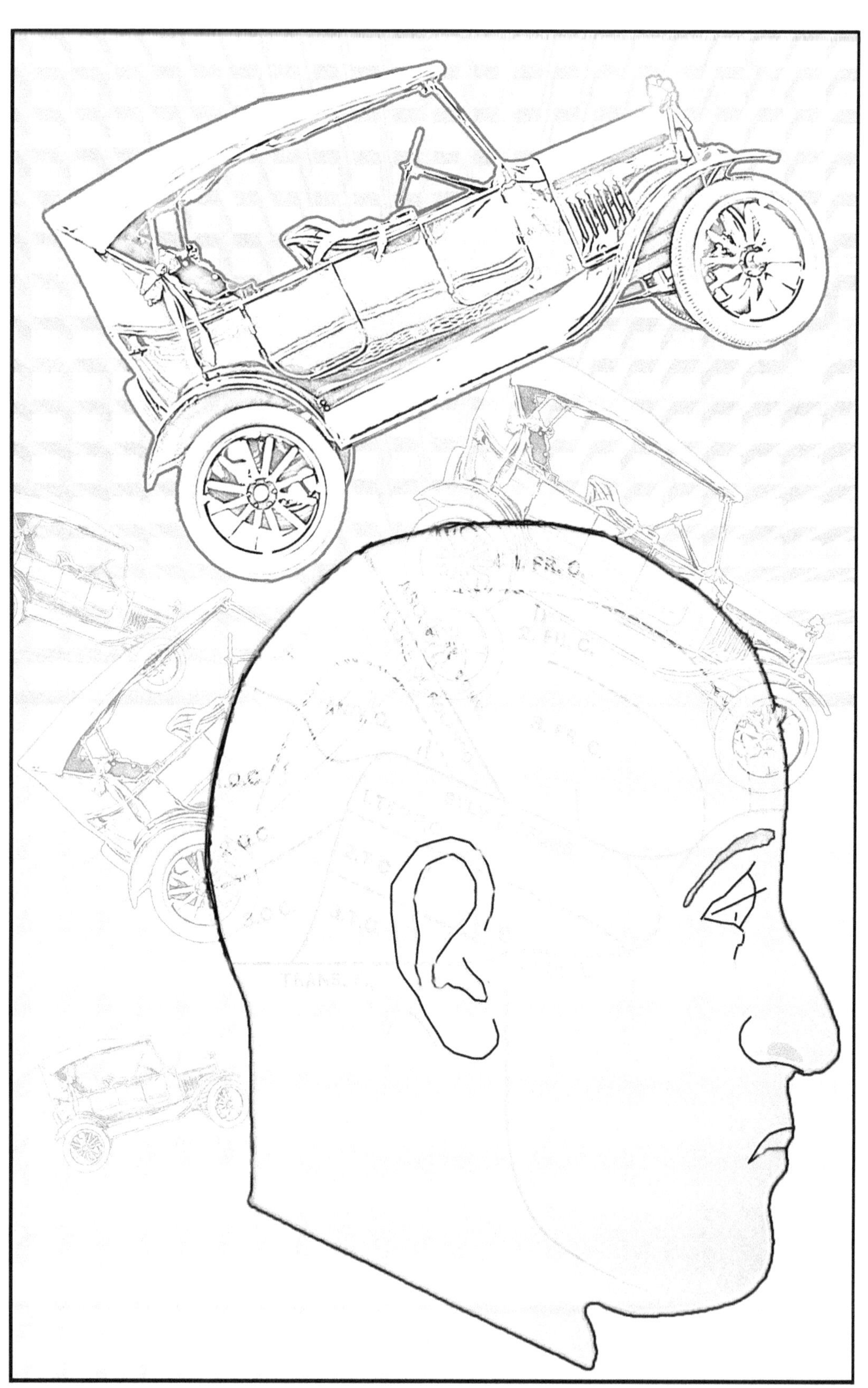

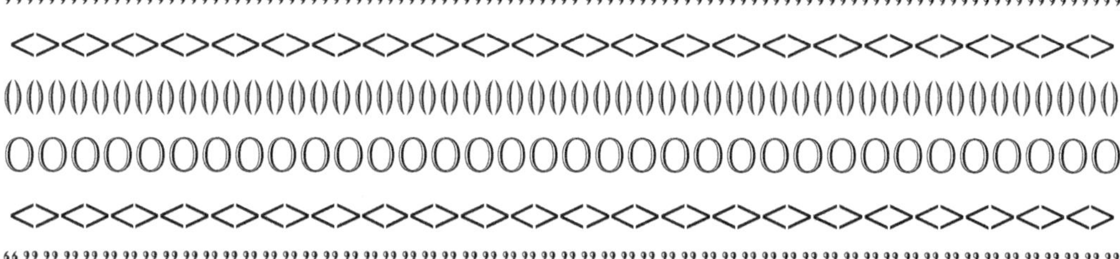

MY MOTHER TOLD ME TO BE A LADY. AND FOR HER, THAT MEANT BE YOUR OWN PERSON, BE INDEPENDENT.

--- RUTH BADER GINSBURG, speaking in a 2002 "Morning Edition" radio interview with Nina Totenberg.

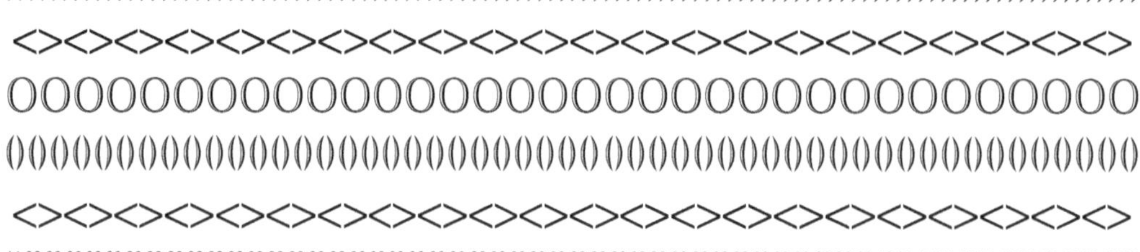

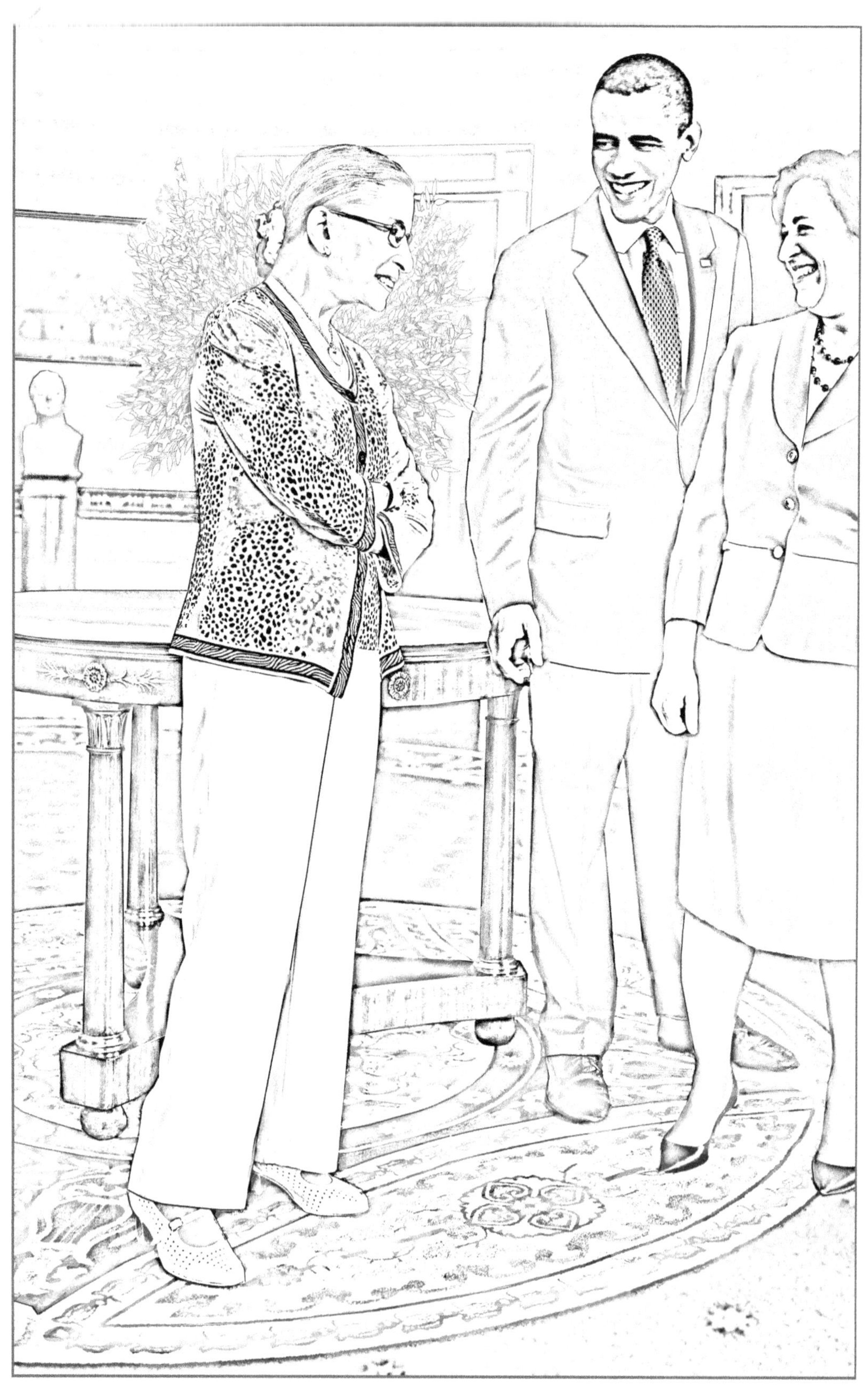

88888888888888888888888888888888888888888888888888888888888888888888888888888888888888888888888888888888
OOOOOOOOOOOOOOOOOOOOOOOOOOOOOOOOOOOOOOOOOOOOOOOOOOOOOOOOOOOOOO
88888888888888888888888888888888888888888888888888888888888888888888888888888888888888888888888888888888

I DON'T REALLY LIVE ON COMPLIMENTS. AS A MATTER OF FACT, THEY HAVE A WAY OF DISTRACTING ME. I KNOW A WHOLE LOT OF MUSICIANS, ARTISTS OUT THERE WHO HEARS THE COMPLIMENTS AND THINKS "WOW, I MUST HAVE BEEN REALLY GREAT" AND SO THEY GET FAT AND SATISFIED AND THEY GET LOST.

--- JIMI HENDRIX: interviewed on The Dick Cavett Show, 9-9-1969

88888888888888888888888888888888888888888888888888888888888888888888888888888888888888888888888888888888
OOOOOOOOOOOOOOOOOOOOOOOOOOOOOOOOOOOOOOOOOOOOOOOOOOOOOOOOOOOOOO
88888888888888888888888888888888888888888888888888888888888888888888888888888888888888888888888888888888

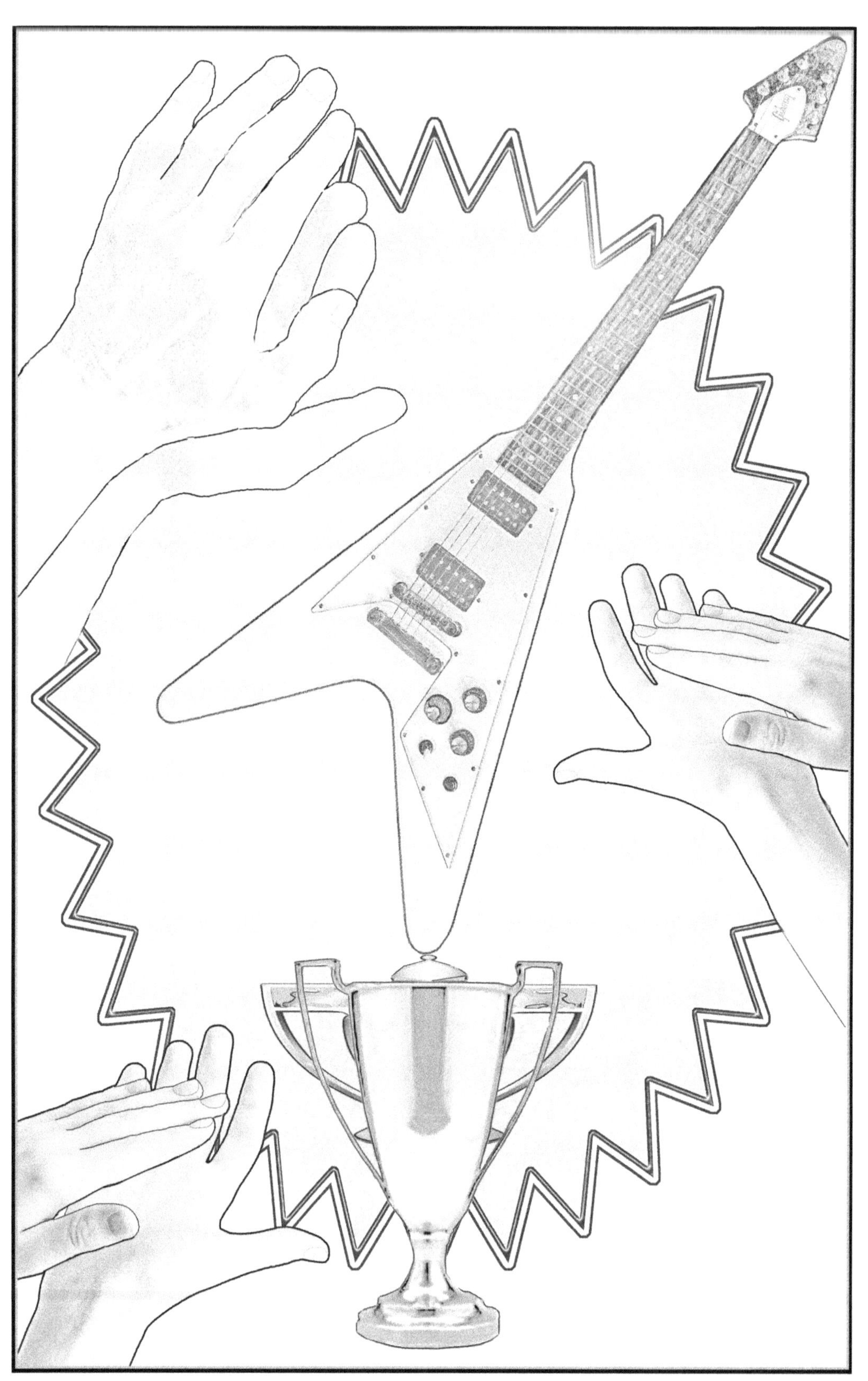

THROUGH TRAVEL I FIRST BECAME AWARE OF THE OUTSIDE WORLD; IT WAS THROUGH TRAVEL THAT I FOUND MY OWN INTROSPECTIVE WAY INTO BECOMING A PART OF IT.

--- EUDORA WELTY: One Writer's Beginnings, 1983, page 76

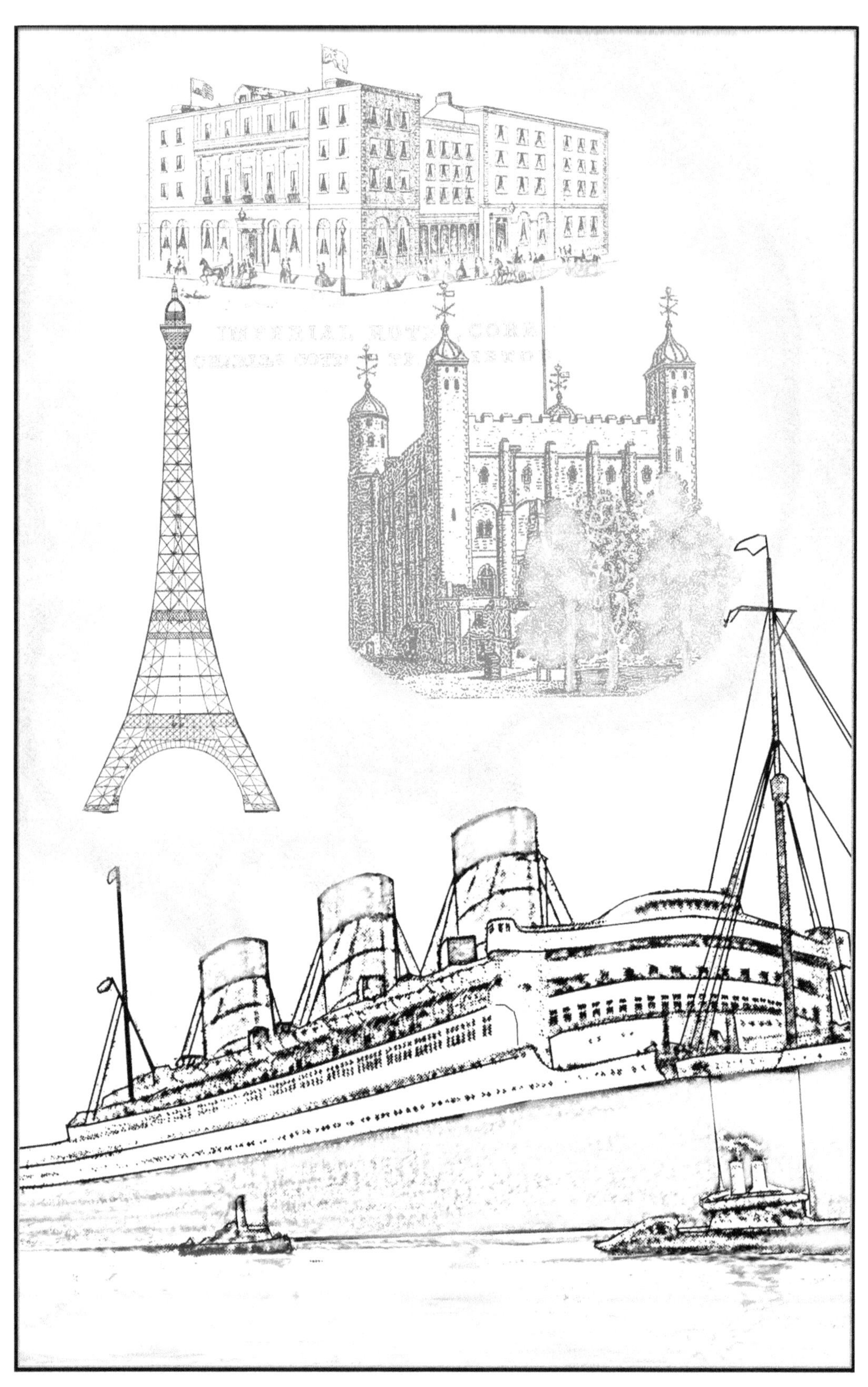

IF YOU CAN EXAMINE AND FACE YOUR LIFE, YOU CAN DISCOVER THE TERMS WITH WHICH YOU ARE CONNECTED TO OTHER LIVES, AND THEY CAN DISCOVER THEM, TOO — THE TERMS WITH WHICH THEY ARE CONNECTED TO OTHER PEOPLE.

--- JAMES BALDWIN: "An interview with James Baldwin" (1961); an interview with Studs Terkel published in Conversations With James Baldwin (1989)

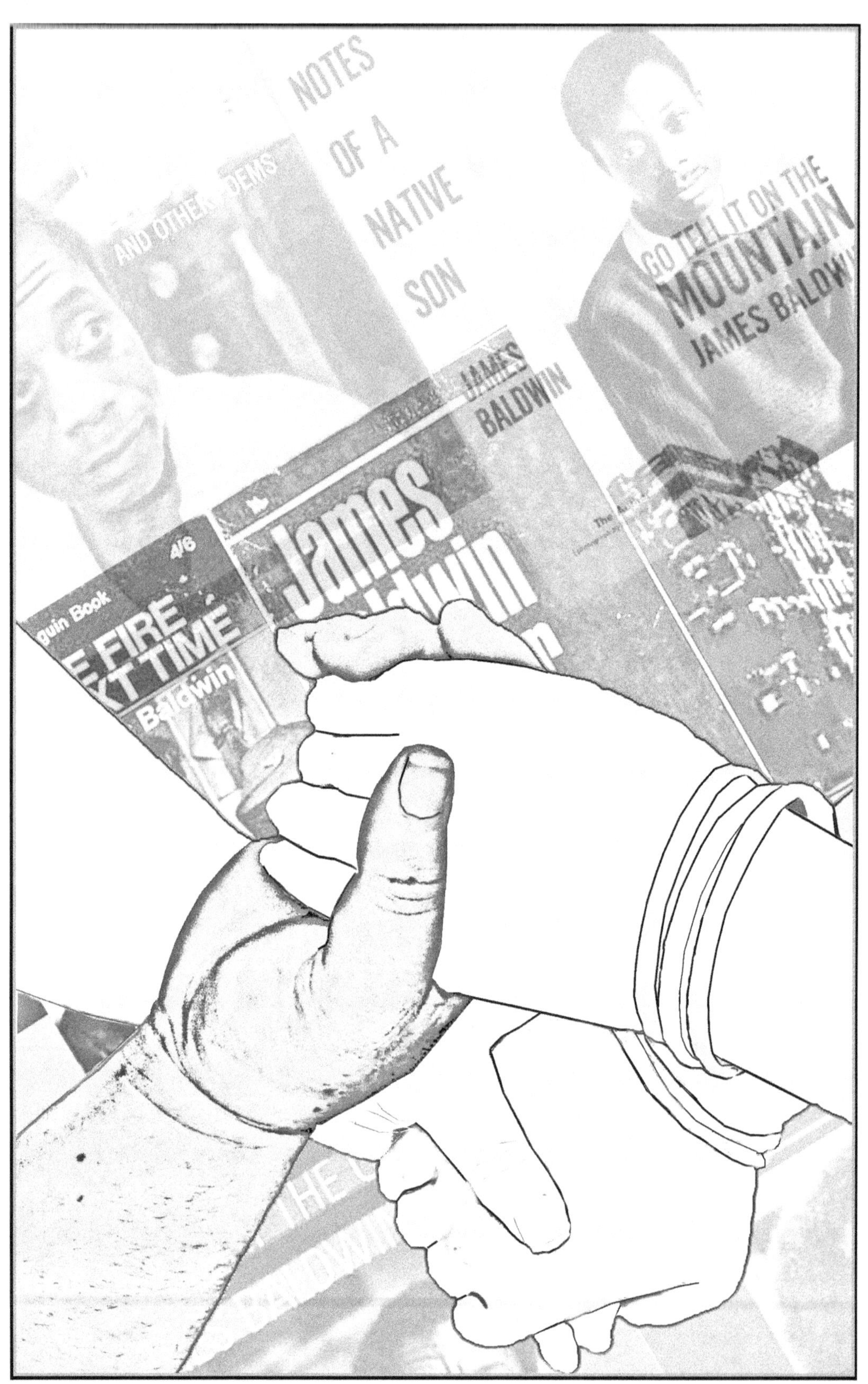
NOTES
OF A
NATIVE
SON
JAMES
BALDWIN
GO TELL IT ON THE
MOUNTAIN
JAMES BALDWIN
James
4/6
Baldwin

HOW DO WE KNOW THE PAIN OR ANOTHER'S EARLIER YEARS ... A LOT OF LEEWAY IS NEEDED FOR THE OTHER – YET HOW MUCH IS UNHEALTHY FOR ONE TO BEAR. I THINK TO LOVE BRAVELY IS THE BEST AND ACCEPT – AS MUCH AS ONE CAN BEAR.

– MARILYN MONROE: from Marilyn's personal diaries in 1958, in Fragments: Poems, Intimate Notes, Letters. Ed. by Stanley Buchthal and Bernard Comment.

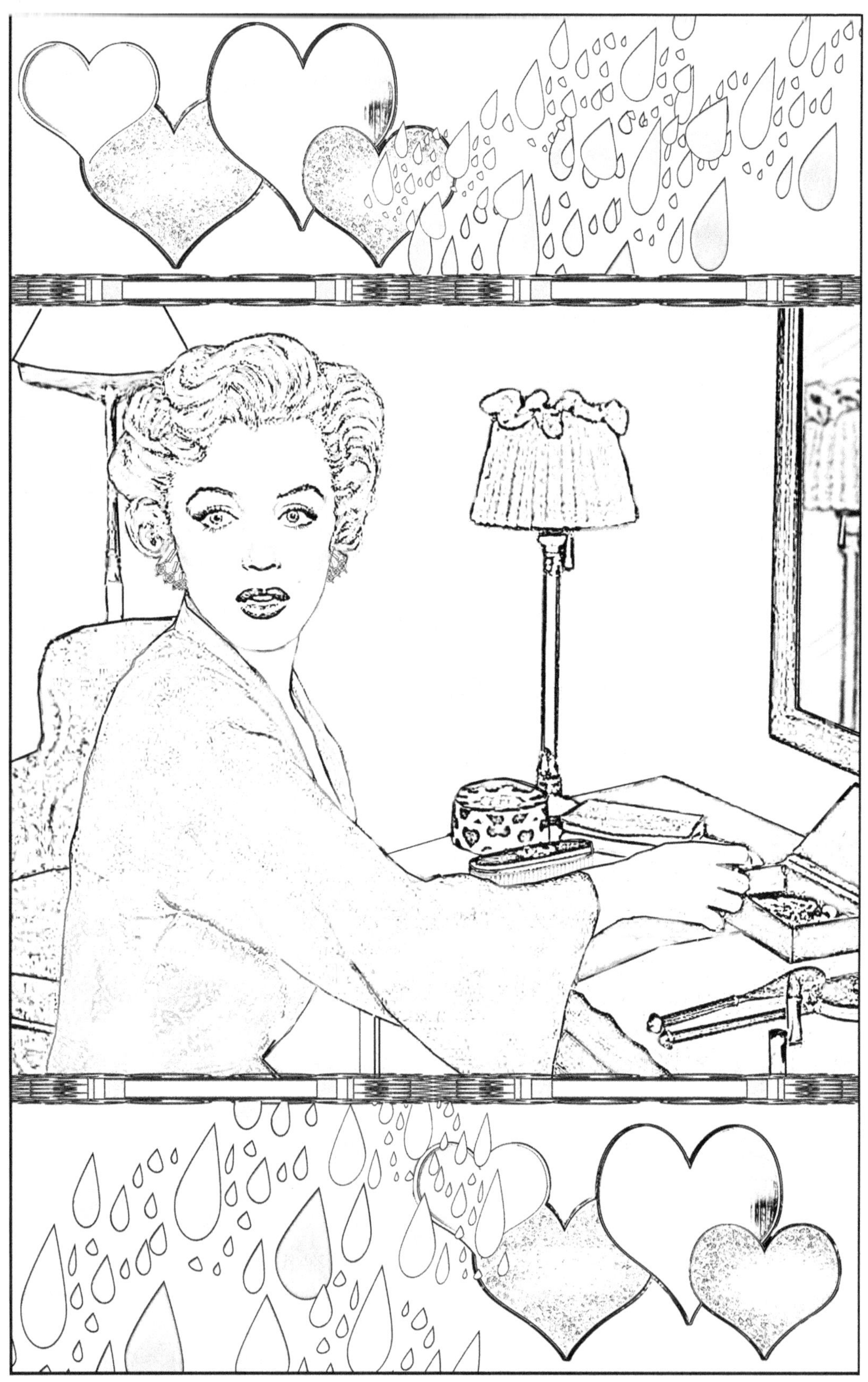

THE WAY A TEAM PLAYS AS A WHOLE DETERMINES ITS SUCCESS. YOU MAY HAVE THE GREATEST BUNCH OF INDIVIDUAL STARS IN THE WORLD, BUT IF THEY DON'T PLAY TOGETHER, THE CLUB WON'T BE WORTH A DIME.

--- BABE RUTH: As quoted in Great Quotes to Inspire Great Teachers (2001) by Noah ben Shea, p. 39

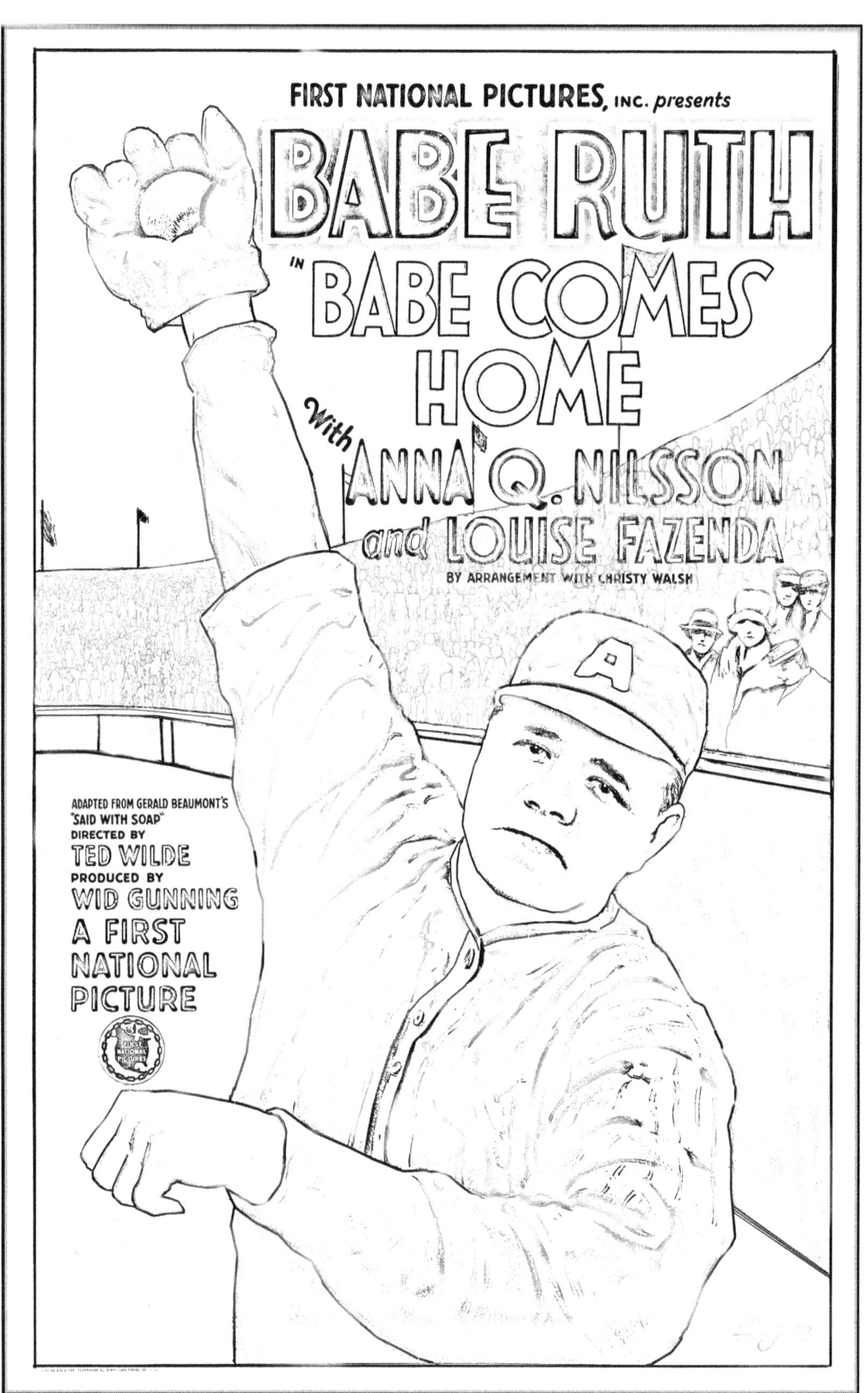
FIRST NATIONAL PICTURES, INC. presents
BABE RUTH
in "BABE COMES HOME"
with ANNA Q. NILSSON
and LOUISE FAZENDA
BY ARRANGEMENT WITH CHRISTY WALSH
A
ADAPTED FROM GERALD BEAUMONT'S
"SAID WITH SOAP"
DIRECTED BY
TED WILDE
PRODUCED BY
WID GUNNING
A FIRST
NATIONAL
PICTURE
FIRST NATIONAL PICTURES

WHEN ONE DOOR OF HAPPINESS CLOSES, ANOTHER OPENS; BUT OFTEN WE LOOK SO LONG AT THE CLOSED DOOR THAT WE DO NOT SEE THE ONE WHICH HAS BEEN OPENED FOR US.

– HELEN KELLER: We Bereaved (1929)

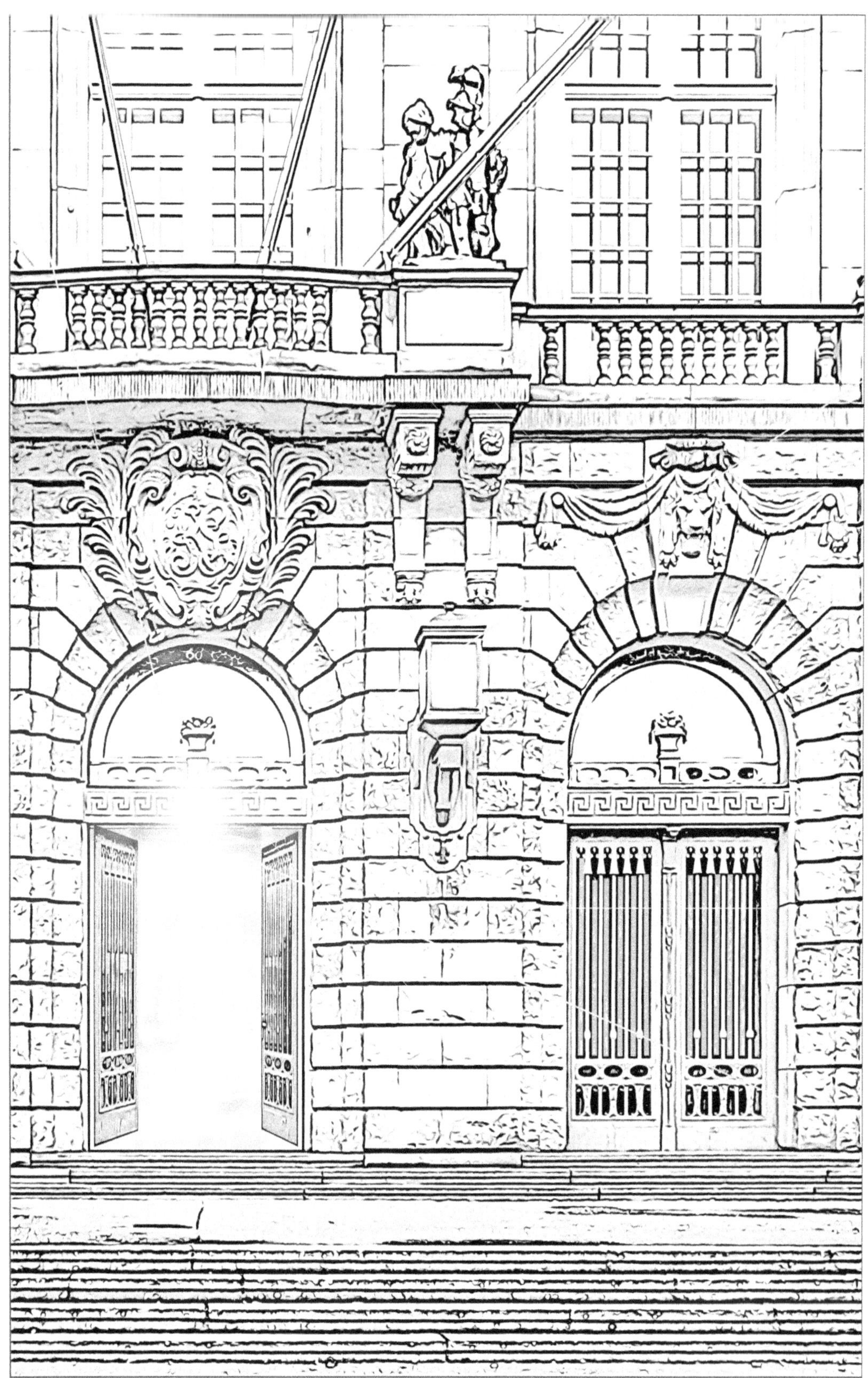

8888888888888888888888888888888888888888888888888888888888888888888888888888888888888888888888
OOOOOOOOOOOOOOOOOOOOOOOOOOOOOOOOOOOOOOOOOOOOOOOOOOOOOOOOOOOOOOO
8888888888888888888888888888888888888888888888888888888888888888888888888888888888888888888888

THE THING TO KNOW IS THAT YOU HAVE DONE A GOOD JOB, THEN IT DOESN'T HURT TO BE CRITICIZED. MY PRESS AGENT WAS VERY INDIGNANT OVER SOMETHING WRITTEN ABOUT ME NOT TOO LONG AGO. "LOOK," I TOLD HIM. "I'VE KNOWN THIS CHARACTER FOR MANY YEARS, AND THE FAULTS HE SEES IN ME ARE REALLY THE FAULTS IN HIMSELF THAT HE HATES."

--- CARY GRANT: from "Love – That's All Cary Grant Ever Thinks About" by Sheilah Graham Westbrook in Motion Picture (June 1964)

8888888888888888888888888888888888888888888888888888888888888888888888888888888888888888888888
OOOOOOOOOOOOOOOOOOOOOOOOOOOOOOOOOOOOOOOOOOOOOOOOOOOOOOOOOOOOOOO
8888888888888888888888888888888888888888888888888888888888888888888888888888888888888888888888

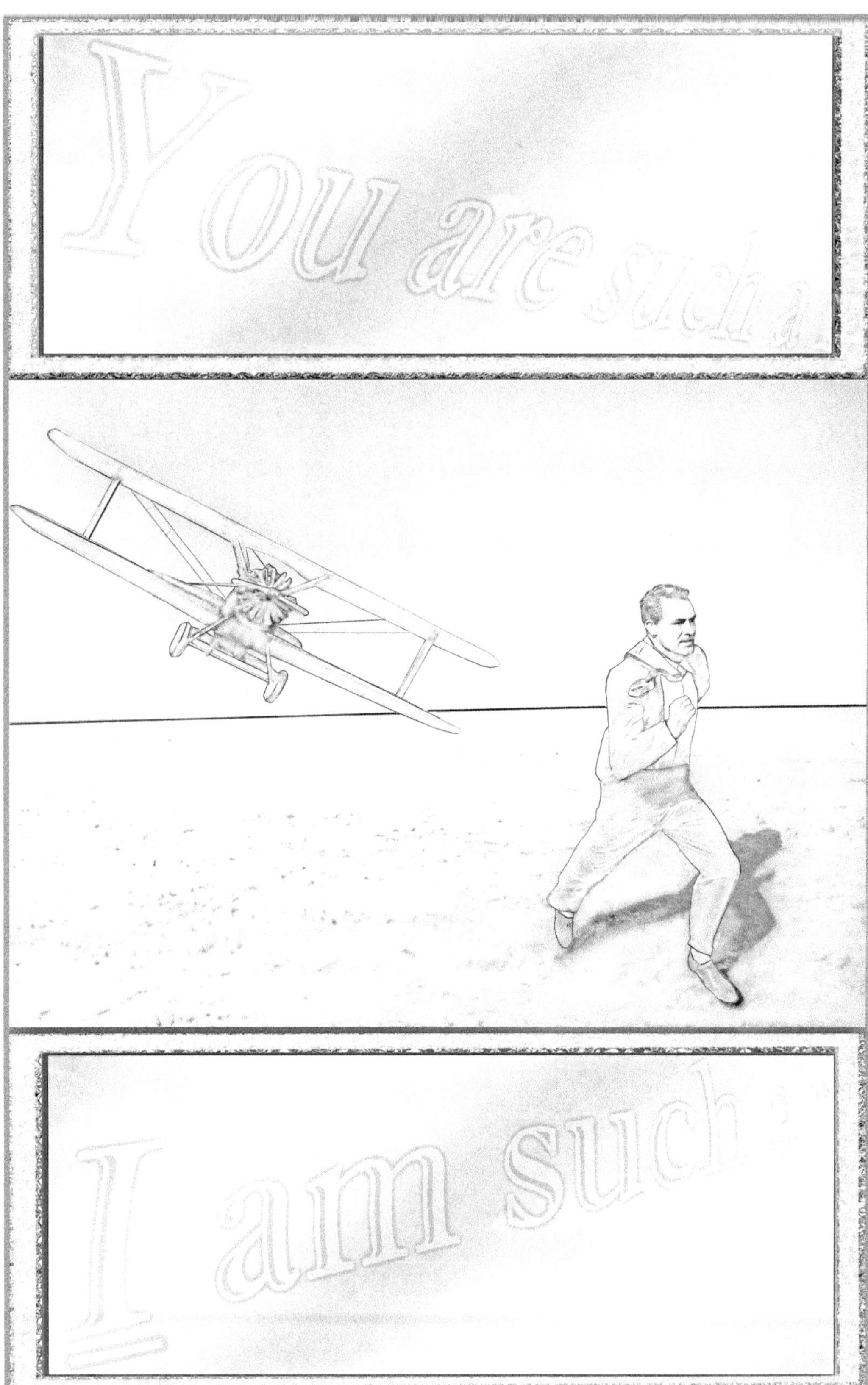

You are such a
I am such

YOU MUST NOT LOSE FAITH IN HUMANITY. HUMANITY IS AN OCEAN; IF A FEW DROPS OF THE OCEAN ARE DIRTY, THE OCEAN DOES NOT BECOME DIRTY.

--- MOHANDAS K. GANDHI: quoted in Gandhi: His Life and Message for the World (1954), by Louis Fischer, p. 177

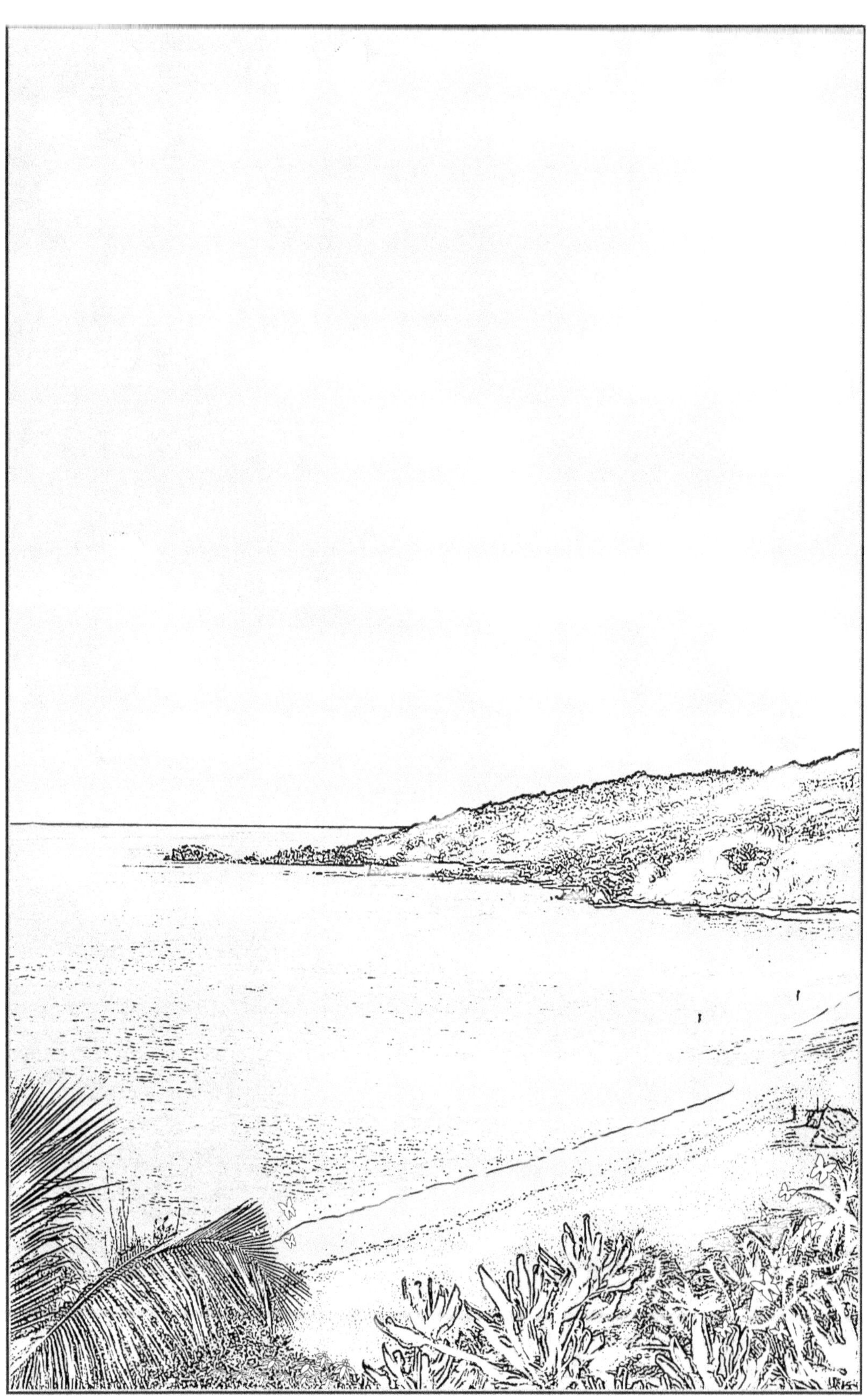

HAVING LIVED LONG, I HAVE EXPERIENCED MANY INSTANCES OF BEING OBLIGED ... TO CHANGE OPINIONS ... WHICH I ONCE THOUGHT RIGHT.

--- BENJAMIN FRANKLIN: Speech in the Constitutional Convention, Philadelphia, Pennsylvania (September 17, 1787); reported in James Madison, *Journal of the Federal Convention*, ed. E. H. Scott (1893), p. 741

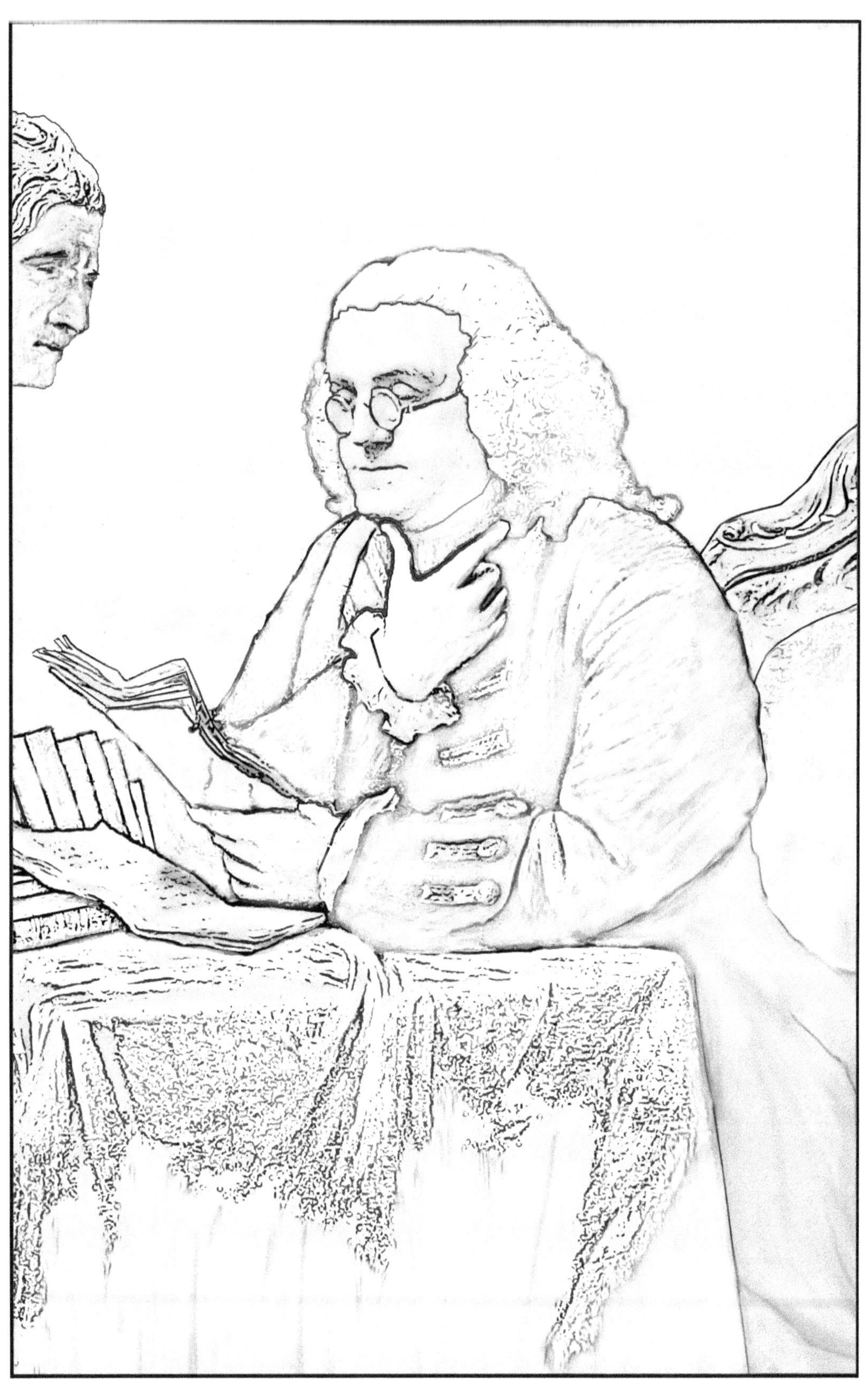

EVERYTHING IN YOUR LIFE IS HAPPENING TO TEACH YOU MORE ABOUT YOURSELF SO EVEN IN A CRISIS, BE GRATEFUL. WHEN DISAPPOINTED, BE GRATEFUL. WHEN THINGS AREN'T GOING THE WAY YOU WANT THEM TO, BE GRATEFUL THAT YOU HAVE SENSE ENOUGH TO TURN IT AROUND.

--- OPRAH WINFREY: Commencement speech at Howard University (12 May 2007)

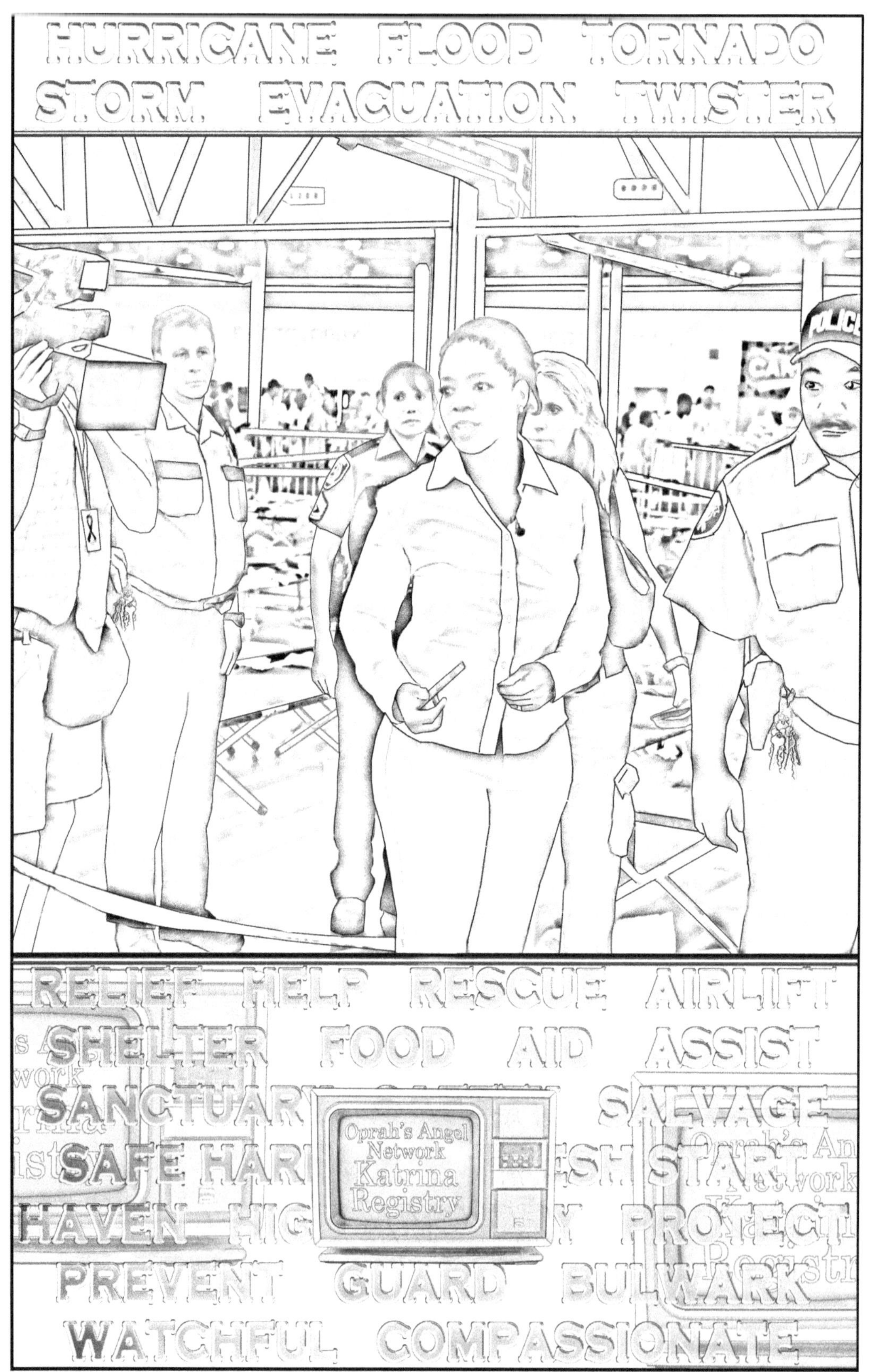
HURRICANE FLOOD TORNADO
STORM EVACUATION TWISTER
RELIEF HELP RESCUE AIRLIFT
SHELTER FOOD AID ASSIST
SALVAGE
Oprah's Angel Network Katrina Registry
HAVEN
PREVENT GUARD BULWARK
WATCHFUL COMPASSIONATE

THINK OF THE POWER OF THE UNIVERSE — TURNING THE EARTH, GROWING THE TREES. THAT'S THE SAME POWER WITHIN YOU — IF YOU'LL ONLY HAVE THE COURAGE AND THE WILL TO USE IT.

--- CHARLIE CHAPLIN: Calvero's answer to Terry's question: "What is there to fight for?" in Chaplin's Limelight (1952)

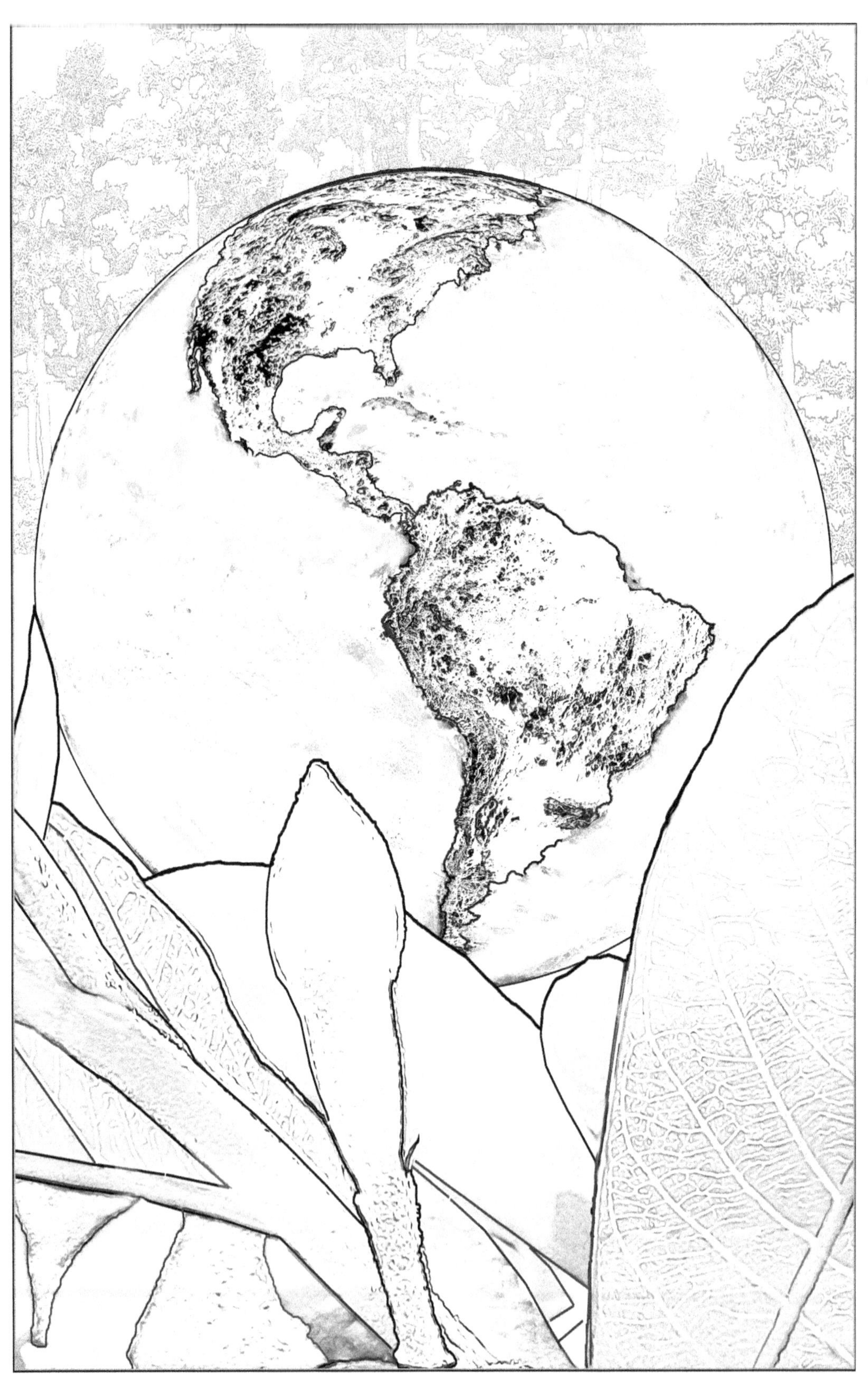

CREDITS

As with *Wise Words from Shakespeare*, in this book I wanted to incorporate authentic historical elements into my pictures. The excellent resources to be found at Wikimedia Commons (commons.wikimedia.org) were my mainstay. In a few cases I used recognizable pieces of the graphics; in others I used components so small or disguised by my reworking that they probably can't be identified. Nevertheless, I want to acknowledge the use of all. These credits appear in the order of the pictures in this book.

COVER: "Colored-Pencils" by Evan-Amos - Own work. Licensed under Public Domain via Wikimedia Commons - https://commons.wikimedia.org/wiki/File:Colored-Pencils.jpg#/media/File:Colored-Pencils.jpg
AND
"Malachite dish (Russia, 19 c)" by shakko - Own work. Licensed under CC BY-SA 3.0 via Wikimedia Commons -
https://commons.wikimedia.org/wiki/File:Malachite_dish_(Russia,_19_c).jpg#/media/File:Malachite_dish_(Russia,_19_c).jpg
AND
VICTORIA: IN CORONATION ROBES (painting by Sir George Hayter): By Henry Pierce Bone - Royal Collection RCIN 422373, Public Domain,
https://commons.wikimedia.org/w/index.php?curid=636543

1-EINSTEIN: CHILDREN: By Cpl. Tyler J. Bolken -
https://www.dvidshub.net/image/675670, Public Domain,
https://commons.wikimedia.org/w/index.php?curid=39562619
AND
EINSTEIN EQUATIONS: By Einstein (gravitational) field equations including the cosmological constant by Albert Einstein from his theory of general relativity (Stephen Weinberg, Gravitation and cosmology, New York, 1972 p. 155); painting by Jan-Willem Bruins (TegenBeeld); photograph by Vysotsky - Own work, CC BY-SA 4.0,
https://commons.wikimedia.org/w/index.php?curid=50130596
AND
MUSEUM: By MartinThoma - Own work, CC0, https://commons.wikimedia.org/w/index.php?curid=33940296

2- GARLAND: 1943 film "Presenting Lily Mars". By Metro-Goldwyn-Mayer (MGM).
http://www.imdb.com/video/screenplay/vi631046425/ trailer, Public Domain,
https://commons.wikimedia.org/w/index.php?curid=4997290

3- MOZART: VIENNA STATUE: By © Hubertl / Wikimedia Commons /, CC BY-SA 4.0,
https://commons.wikimedia.org/w/index.php?curid=40108191
AND
SHEET MUSIC: Das Veilchen: By Wolfgang Amadeus Mozart - Leopold Schmidt: Mozart, Schlesische Verlagsanstalt Berlin, 1920, n. S. 80, Public Domain,
https://commons.wikimedia.org/w/index.php?curid=30204499

4- VICTORIA: IN CORONATION ROBES (painting by Sir George Hayter): By Henry Pierce Bone - Royal Collection RCIN 422373, Public Domain, https://commons.wikimedia.org/w/index.php?curid=636543

5- TRUMAN: SIGN: Buckstopsherefrontsmall.jpg Uploaded: 18 April 2007 Public Domain, https://commons.wikimedia.org/w/index.php?curid=1964883
AND
WHITE HOUSE: By U.S. Federal Government - Extracted from PDF version of a 2003 progress report (direct PDF URL http://www.whitehouse.gov/)., Public Domain, https://commons.wikimedia.org/w/index.php?curid=3535200

6- RUSSELL: 1966 game: (Note that Wilt Chamberlain wears a mask due to an injury.) By New York World-Telegram and the Sun staff photographer - Library of Congress Prints and Photographs Division. New York World-Telegram and the Sun Newspaper Photograph Collection. http://hdl.loc.gov/loc.pnp/cph.3c15430, Public Domain, https://commons.wikimedia.org/w/index.php?curid=8827832
AND
Color version: By Wilt_Chamberlain_Bill_Russell.jpg: New York World-Telegram and the Sun staff photographerderivative work: Sportingn (talk) - Wilt_Chamberlain_Bill_Russell.jpg, Public Domain, https://commons.wikimedia.org/w/index.php?curid=10300532
AND
BASKETBALL: By Reisio - Own work, Public Domain, https://commons.wikimedia.org/w/index.php?curid=542943

7- CARROLL: CAT, COURT: By John Tenniel - pdf from gasl.org, Public Domain, https://commons.wikimedia.org/w/index.php?curid=1491695 Public Domain File:De Alice's Abenteuer im Wunderland Carroll pic 31.jpg Created: 31 December 1868
STATS, GRAPHS:
By William Playfair - The Commercial and Political Atlas, 1786 (3th ed. edition 1801), Public Domain, https://commons.wikimedia.org/w/index.php?curid=42808904
AND
By Felix O - A Cumberland Bus service, CC BY-SA 2.0, https://commons.wikimedia.org/w/index.php?curid=17544154
AND
By Xpicto at Polish Wikipedia, CC BY-SA 3.0, https://commons.wikimedia.org/w/index.php?curid=2990152

8- CURIE: CURIE: By Vitold Muratov - Scan and digitalisation of illustration out of "Welt im Umbruch 1900-1914". Verlag Das Beste GmbH.Stuttgart.1999 ISBN 3870708379 2011-11-20, CC BY-SA 3.0, https://commons.wikimedia.org/w/index.php?curid=17428877
AND
TEST TUBES: By Morten Bisgaard - From the book "Opfindelsernes Bog" 1878 by André Lütken, Public Domain, https://commons.wikimedia.org

9- FORD: Cranio: By Unknown - Popular Science Monthly Volume 37, Public Domain, https://commons.wikimedia.org/w/index.php?curid=11857439
AND
Thinker: By Ibex73 - Own work, CC BY-SA 4.0, https://commons.wikimedia.org/w/index.php?curid=47609901
AND

Model T: By Jarek Tuszynski / CC-BY-SA-3.0, CC BY-SA 3.0, https://commons.wikimedia.org/w/index.php?curid=27671884

10- BADER GINSBURG: (Note the presence of another left-hander, President Barack Obama, in the original photo; Justice Elena Kagan is the third person present.) Oval Office: By The White House from Washington, DC - P080610PS-0595, Public Domain, https://commons.wikimedia.org/w/index.php?curid=12354624

11- HENDRIX: GIBSON FLYING V GUITAR: By Monika Fischer - ASH_2015_FlyingV01, CC BY-SA 2.0, https://commons.wikimedia.org/w/index.php?curid=42193013
AND
TROPHY 1: By The authors of the image above, edited by GARDEN - Derived from :File:Trophy.png., Public Domain,
https://commons.wikimedia.org/w/index.php?curid=19013192
AND
TROPHY 2: By Riccardo de Conciliis - Own work, CC BY-SA 2.5,
https://commons.wikimedia.org/w/index.php?curid=37583275
AND 2 Pairs of clapping hands:
-- By Niklas Bildhauer, Germany. - Own work, CC BY-SA 3.0,
https://commons.wikimedia.org/w/index.php?curid=5565344
-- By Evan-Amos - Own work, CC BY-SA 3.0,
https://commons.wikimedia.org/w/index.php?curid=18956740

12- WELTY: POSTCARD OF THE CUNARD WHITE STAR RMS "QUEEN MARY," by Cunard - Postcards from the Early 1920s, Public Domain,
https://commons.wikimedia.org/w/index.php?curid=30481391
AND
EIFFEL TOWER: By E. Monod - L'Exposition universelle de 1889, Public Domain,
https://commons.wikimedia.org/w/index.php?curid=41546460
AND
TOWER OF LONDON: By Grose Francis - http://www.fromoldbooks.org/Grose-Antiquities-VolIII/pages/141-tower-of-london/Grose, Francis: "The Antiquities of England and Wales (Vol III)" (1783), Public Domain, https://commons.wikimedia.org/w/index.php?curid=1961276
AND
IRISH HOTEL: By Image extracted from page 229 of The new Hand-Book of Ireland; an illustrated guide for tourists and travellers, by GODKIN, James - and WALKER (John A.). Original held and digitised by the British Library. This file is from the Mechanical Curator collection, a set of over 1 million images scanned from out-of-copyright books and released to Flickr Commons by the British Library. Public Domain,
https://commons.wikimedia.org/w/index.php?curid=36711007

13- BALDWIN: HANDS: By Vicki Nunn - Own work, Public Domain,
https://commons.wikimedia.org/w/index.php?curid=12075924
AND
BOOK COVER PORTIONS under Fair Use Doctrine:
http://thethoughtfox.co.uk/wp-content/uploads/sites/4/2013/07/james_baldwin_books.jpg
http://d.gr-assets.com/books/1347513316l/38459.jpg
http://www.derringerbooks.com/derringer/images/items/003074.jpg
http://media.npr.org/assets/bakertaylor/covers/j/jimmys-blues-and-other-poems/9780807084861_custom-70350c0dfa40aeac7776670f9e7b95ff

14- MONROE: SCENE FROM "Don't Bother to Knock": By Dell Publications, Inc. New York, publisher of Modern Screen - Page 33, Public Domain, https://commons.wikimedia.org/w/index.php?curid=49827932

15- RUTH: MOVIE POSTER: Ruth took time off in 1927 to star with Anna Q. Nilsson in this First National silent production "Babe Comes Home". This film is now lost. By Unknown - ha.com, Public Domain, https://commons.wikimedia.org/w/index.php?curid=31405822

16- KELLER: DOORS: Berlin Kammergericht; by Ansgar Koreng / CC BY-SA 3.0 (DE), CC BY-SA 3.0 de, https://commons.wikimedia.org/w/index.php?curid=36124504

17- GRANT: SCENE from "North by Northwest"-- Public Domain, https://commons.wikimedia.org/w/index.php?curid=465607

18- GANDHI: INDIAN OCEAN, Grand Anse beach on island of La Digue, Seychelles : By Tobias Alt, Tobi 87 - Own work, GFDL, https://commons.wikimedia.org/w/index.php?curid=3827045

19- FRANKLIN: 1767 PAINTING: Franklin with bust of Isaac Newton. By David Martin - The White House Historical Association, Public Domain, https://commons.wikimedia.org/w/index.php?curid=9390044

20- WINFREY: OPRAH IN TEXAS, POST-HURRICANE KATRINA: By Andrea Booher - This image is from the FEMA Photo Library., Public Domain, https://commons.wikimedia.org/w/index.php?curid=8079449
AND
OLD TELEVISION: By Solomon203 - Own work, CC BY-SA 4.0, https://commons.wikimedia.org/w/index.php?curid=43303439

21- CHAPLIN: EARTH: By NASA/ GSFC/ NOAA/ USGS - http://antwrp.gsfc.nasa.gov/apod/image/0304/bluemarble2k_big.jpg, Public Domain, https://commons.wikimedia.org/w/index.php?curid=3416826
AND:
BACKGROUND TREES: By Ragesoss - Own work, CC BY-SA 3.0, https://commons.wikimedia.org/w/index.php?curid=4508680
AND:
FOREGROUND FOLIAGE: By Fqamar - Own work, Public Domain, https://commons.wikimedia.org/w/index.php?curid=5157893

....

ABOUT THE AUTHOR

K. Sherrerd Lowry, Ph.D., received a doctorate degree in Mathematics Education in 2006. Classroom teaching, a stint editing mathematics textbooks for a major publisher, and a love of story—combined with an abiding interest in the graphic arts—have resulted in the children's math storybooks *LC4A and the Big Test* and *Surprises for Zu-Zu: A Rhyming Counting Book*. Both are available as ebooks from Kindle.

LC4A is aimed at students who experience difficulties in solving word problems. It is also available in a paperback version as an omnibus coloring book/workbook/storybook, with expanded problem sets and a Parents' Guide, from CreateSpace and from Amazon. (The title of that version is: *LC4A and the Big Test: A Math-Story Planet Workbook.*)

Other books by the author include both ebook and paper editions of *Grey Fairy/White Wolf: Three Classic Lang Tales Retold* (both with illustrations by the author), and an ebook about communicating online: *FORUM FINESSE: A Guide to Impact and Influence in Online Talk.*

A coloring book for adults, *Wise Words from Shakespeare*, is the first in the series that includes the present volume. The series offers inspiring quotations illustrated by pictures that go beyond the traditional children's coloring book staples (black lines outlining white spaces) to offer gray lines and modeling. The result is a work of both substance and pictorial richness that any colorist will be pleased to complete.

Comment on the K. Sherrerd Lowry Amazon Author page, and check out upcoming offerings at the Duer Press website, http://duerpress.com/

Your feedback is welcome.

www.ingramcontent.com/pod-product-compliance
Lightning Source LLC
LaVergne TN
LVHW061930110826
845155LV00053B/207

* 9 7 8 1 9 4 5 9 3 9 0 0 6 *